WHAT'S AN AMERICAN DOING HERE?

REFLECTIONS ON TRAVEL

IN THE THIRD WORLD

"The world is a book and those who do not travel read only one page."

—St. Augustine

By Stanley C. Diamond

Eloquent Books

Eloquent Books
An imprint of Strategic Book Group
P.O. Box 333
Durham CT 06422
www.StrategicBookGroup.com

ISBN: 978-1-60911-659-0

TABLE OF CONTENTS

ACKNOWLEDGEMENTS

Most of the adventures and memories described here would have been impossible without the partnership of my devoted, intrepid wife, Beverly. I thank her for that as well as for her reading of the book and her recollection of incidents which seeped out of my recall over the many years of our travel. I appreciate the effort that my friends, Elaine Dushoff and Janet Waxman, expended in their reviews of the writing. And to all my friends and family who have traveled with me at one time or another, thanks for the encouragement and the company. Finally, I offer my gratitude to the many warm and wonderful folks I have encountered on my journeys, both fellow travelers and residents of the lands I have traversed. I have learned so much from all of you.

FOREWORD

I am one of those fortunate people who traveled widely during a lifetime of learning and adventure. On those voyages I worried about my survival while stranded in a flood in the mountains of Western China, attended numerous funerals and weddings in Indonesia and West Africa and other far away locales, been robbed at gunpoint in Guatemala and by trickery in Bolivia, thwarted efforts to pick my pockets in Brazil and Spain, worked and wandered for three years in Italy and Germany, two of the years alone and one with my young family exploring most of the continent of Europe. During that time, I rocked a four poster bed with the chills of dysentery in a small Mexican boarding house, witnessed shamans and witch doctors weaving their spells in Papua New Guinea and in Mayan rituals in Mesoamerica as well as in the fields of remote tribal villages in India, attended Candomble[1] religious rites in Brazil, voodoo ceremonies in Benin and mosques in Pakistan, Morocco, Turkey, India and Egypt, watched elephant led parades at Hindu Pujahs and Periheras, rode in cars that broke down along remote roads, went to Christmas masses in Mexico and Spain and synagogue services in Rome and Romania and South India, gazed at fishermen perched on poles in the water off the Sri Lanka coast and others who rowed their vessels with their feet in Myanmar, ridden camels in the deserts of Mali and the Sinai and the great Camel Fair in Rajasthan, endured wobbly transport on the backs of elephants in India and Africa, and wound up well ahead of my luggage on several trips.

---

1   Candomble is a religious practice centered in Bahia, Brazil. It is derived from African beliefs, especially those of the Yoruba of West Africa, and modified by slaves who were carried to the Bahia area in Brazil. There are about two million followers. The religion seeks harmony with nature and is organized around religious centers known as terreiros, which are usually led by high priestesses, Followers worship a group of orixás. god-like figures in a yearly cycle.

Not only have I been at the scene of numerous memorable and challenging undertakings but, in the course of my travels, I have learned to photograph the places I visited in a way that represents my experiences and to develop programs using my photos and my newly gathered knowledge to help others appreciate what Third World travel is like and to encourage them to consider following in my footsteps if they were physically, emotionally and economically able and were inclined to do so. If my lectures were not always successful in that endeavor, lots of folks in my audiences still learned from and enjoyed these presentations. That has given me much ongoing pleasure – a truly perfect retirement pursuit.

One additional treasure that I have been granted in my lifetime which has helped me see the world up close without hesitation or worry is the woman I married. My wife, Bev, never harbored the dreams of exploration that I possessed for as long as I remember nor had she ever imagined herself a lifelong traveler, yet she turned out to be courageous and flexible and interested in every region we visited and, not only did she support my lust for the journey, but she augmented it by adding her own increasing desire to visit everywhere we could. She turned out to be an excellent traveler and a great sport. Without that good fortune, I would have wandered far fewer miles and traversed less exotic roads in the time I have been given. I hope some of what you read here and some of the photos I have included to illustrate my travels will inspire you to travel to new places and help you gain a greater appreciation of the amazing world so few of us are lucky enough to get to know. I had been fortunate enough to travel alone during the early years and more recently to wander with my family, both of which styles are gratifying and interesting in unique ways, but most of the miles I have traversed were with Bev as we journeyed to exotic places often under strange circumstances. I would not trade that life of travel for a throne or a fortune.

CHAPTER ONE

DISCOVERING THE THIRD WORLD

"Most travelers today may appear on the surface to be just another bunch of men and women with backpacks and dreams of freedom. But underneath there are echoes of ancient Taoist sages and Zen priests, wandering cloud-hidden among the herbs and flowers of silent hills, intent on unlocking wisdom and awareness. By traveling to distant parts of the world we discover hitherto unsuspected parts of our self, or perhaps it is better to say that we find new selves. The traveler who is honest enough with himself about the highs and lows, the fears and ecstasies of journeying through unknown landscapes is equipped to find new treasures within his own psyche. These are the permanent gifts with which he returns home, and which enrich him long after once vivid experiences have turned to dim memories."
—David Yeadon, *The Way of the Wanderer*, pp xiii

In and out of Europe

Back in the nineteen fifties and sixties, traveling in Europe was a rather affordable, easy undertaking for Americans. The continent was rebuilding from the leftover injuries of war and the economies of the area were just beginning to reemerge. That meant that the dollar went a long way for visitors from the multitude of young backpackers roaming about in search of excitement and adventure to mature travelers seeking the beauty of the countryside, walled cities and priceless art treasures. A large part of Europe was substantially off bounds for several post-war decades due to the division between East and West and the limits to freedom of movement that were a facet of the distrust and hostility that characterized what came be called the Cold War. Yet there were plenty of interesting places to go to in Europe and travel was a true bargain during those decades. At the same time, technology had not yet completely reshaped the landscape. There was still a plethora of lovely, traditional areas to wander about in, including virtually all the segments of the eastern part of Europe that were accessible. And there was Iberia that remained at that time a developing section of the continent; there were lovely sites along the Mediterranean shoreline and lots of villages in Central Europe where folk crafts, colorful dress and traditional practices still persisted. It was in that setting that I worked and traveled throughout the continent for more than three years. During two of those years I taught the children of our military who were stationed in post-war Germany. I was single and fancy-free with boundless energy. I followed that rich experience some ten years later with a delightful year of teaching at an international school in Rome while sharing that adventure with my young kids and wife. At the end of that year an extended summer trip through the continent turned out to be a highlight of my life. For over two months we rambled along in the Peugeot station wagon we bought in Italy throughout Western Europe and even a good part of the east with our kids sleeping in the back and all of our belongings in a bag or two. We stopped where we wanted, explored sites few other Americans had visited during the post-war period, and reveled in our wonderful idyll.

Those periods of travel constituted the first really extensive time abroad that I carved out for myself. In order to begin those experiences, I resigned from a very good teaching position without knowing where I would find employment on my return. As it turned out, I was offered the opportunity to continue in my former job after I returned to the States so my anticipated sacrifice never occurred. A full summer journey through Northern Europe with my young family in the seventies required me to forfeit a good and satisfying second job as a camp director. There has never been a moment of regret about any of those decisions. Of course, a lot of luck contributed an ultimately successful outcome. My wife and I still look back on our year in Rome as perhaps the most treasured and intense period of our entire married life.

So what does all that have to do with the Third World? Post-war Europe was my entry into the kind of travel I ultimately came to relish all my life as well as the training ground for my exploration of much of the rest of the world the way I eventually wanted to pursue it – in search of adventure and knowledge.

Twenty-five years passed before I returned to Europe after the summer trip of 1971 and then only because I secured a job as a lecturer aboard an exquisite cruise line. My first cruise made clear to me why I had not returned for such a long time. Though I had visited Venice several times during my earlier European sojourns, a stop there a quarter century later featured wall to wall tourists and long waiting lines to see the highlights; another revisit offered packed museums and parks in Barcelona and a third brought us back to Rome to sip on five dollar cups of coffee in its lovely squares. These return trips reinforced my disinclination to spend much time in contemporary Europe even with the rich sites it offers. There were not many places I had missed on my earlier trips there but bargains I discovered when we were younger were no longer available. As a matter of fact, handiwork, food and other travel expenses were even more expensive than at home. I also realized that visiting ports for a day or less was not the kind of travel that satisfied me even though I did enjoy giving presentations onboard about the glorious cities in which we were stopping. Encounters on shore in the limited time we docked just seemed too rare and too shallow, the days were too rushed, and the sites too populated and busy. I yearned to return to my original style of leisurely wandering, to spend mytime in places where I could mosey about in piazzas or walk along back streets without worrying about when I had to be back on the ship. It was intensive and independent travel, not vacationing, that satisfied my desire to experience the world around me. After three or four laps of luxury sailing, I eventually turned down future offers to ride the waves and decided even cost-free travel had a price tag for me, namely, the time I lost doing what I truly wanted to do. Nonetheless, the opportunity to be treated to the most lavish indulgence of creature comfort and service I could ever imagine on the sumptuous vessels that carried me was one of several unexpected bonuses of the earlier travel I had done.

The Third World

It was 1987 before my wife and I went on our first extended trip together to what is referred to in this book as "The Third World," a term, used commonly after World War Two to designate nations which had not yet developed a high level of industrial and technological growth. Some of these places were countries which had been colonized earlier or were economically dominated by the West. A few others were isolated places which had never shared in the outcomes of the worldwide industrial revolution or more recent technological progress. The term became fairly widely used to distinguish between such nations and those that constituted the Western Bloc during the Cold War (occasionally referred to as the First World) or those aligned with the Soviet Union (Second World). Much of contemporary China, some petroleum rich countries and a few other locales like Brazil are much harder to categorize today but I will use "Third World" to refer to all of the areas which were struggling toward a modern economy in the second half of the 20th century.

Getting Started

My first real opportunity to travel came after my first year of teaching and a regular paycheck. My first time outside the USA as well as my first trip to the Third World was a journey that consisted of a cross-country drive from Philadelphia to Mexico City and back via California. During that extraordinary summer, I lived in a boarding house in Mexico City for two months, got a case of dysentery, met several interesting people, became much more facile in spoken Spanish, and began to realize that traveling was going to be an important activity for me, an ultimately essential part of my life.

I remember yearning to see the world even as a young child. Back in the pre-television era, I recall returning again and again to a *World Book Encyclopedia* that was part of our limited home library; it contained fascinating articles and pictures of exotic places with odd names and people who dressed strangely and had strange customs. The notion that other cultures could be so different from ours captivated me from the start. Later, stamp collecting added to my knowledge and my interest in the world. Colorful pictures from small, Pacific Islands or remote places in South America or Africa filled the pages of my catalogues. Trinidad and Tobago, Azerbaijan, Belgian Congo, Tanganyika, British

Guiana and many more far off places were colorful and mysterious names in the wonderfully diverse assortment of countries and islands in this world. I decided I wanted to see all of them. When it came time to choose my college courses many years later, I found myself most fascinated by cultural anthropology. After a few courses in that discipline I still felt uneasy about the notion of sleeping on dirt floors in remote villages or drinking and eating what the people there did as I pictured anthropologists doing. Somehow a dinner of insects or guinea pigs, scorpions or lizards was just not appealing to me. I have never even been fond of beans. With all of my travel, I confess that such treats are still far from tempting. My creature comfort needs kept me from choosing a career in anthropology although I envied those who did study traditional societies and I appreciated what I learned from their books and their lectures. I loosened up a bit in several aspects of my resistance to going native as I went along but I am still not the most open or adventurous eater even to this day. A little snake or alligator or such is manageable but I do tend to avoid meals that are moving on the plate. No anthropologist am I.

Life Changes

I did not realize how important my summer trip to Mexico would be when I undertook it during the summer following my first year of teaching. It is only in retrospect that I appreciate that at least three important things actually changed me on that trip. First of all, though I did not sleep in villages, I did put myself in a situation where many of the usual concerns- ensuring my personal safety, customary creature comforts, familiar foods, reliable friends, etc. - were simply not available to me. I did not care. I had set out to meet a challenge and I not only did so but found myself exhilarated by the undertaking. It was not a relaxing or pleasant matter to lie in bed with dysentery attended by a first year Panamanian medical student and fellow boarder and hear him diagnose my condition as malaria. But it turned out he was wrong; the fever and chills caused by the dysentery I had actually contracted subsided after a couple of days, and I was able to continue with my trip. I had survived without panic or rescue. A regimen of antibiotics did the trick. Though my legs were unsteady for a couple of days my travel capacity returned shortly after I recovered and I was able to take care of myself in a strange place with relatively little support. That is an essential thing to learn about oneself! Those of us who never come to realize our potential in this respect are forever handicapped by the absence of that realization, but more about that later.

The second happening of that summer that is indelibly inscribed into my being was also life-changing and completely unplanned. It was truly an epiphany. On a beach in a poor section of Acapulco, I met an attractive young woman and entered into a daylong romantic relationship with her. We spent the evening together after which I insisted that I walk her back home in spite of her seeming lack of eagerness to have me do so. As we approached where she lived, I entered an alien world, one I was quite unfamiliar with until that evening. I walked through a desperately impoverished, rural area. Sewage seeped along the side of unpaved paths; people dotted the fields under tents or tin roofs erected to protect them from the rain if they were even lucky enough to have such shelter. I saw no signs of electricity or fresh water sources. Kids cried constantly, most likely from hunger. This was where my date that evening lived. I walked to the tent which housed her and her mother to whom she introduced me, said goodbye (I was leaving the next morning) and slowly made my way back toward the modest hotel where I was staying. Along the way, the horror of what I had seen worked its way inside me. The impact of the evening was reinforced as I stepped by a 10 year old youngster sleeping in the doorway of the hotel where I lodged. At some magical moment, I silently committed myself to work toward the elimination of such conditions for the rest of my life. It is for others to judge how well I have kept that promise, but I know I have remained consciously dedicated to that path ever since that evening. My political activity, my volunteer work, my charitable contributions all reflect in some way or other the conclusions I reached during my walk in Acapulco. Those commitments were reinforced later when I encountered similar or even worse poverty on many future forays into the less fortunate recesses of the world.

One more occurrence, the significance of which only struck me later on, was the joy I had discovered in learning to communicate with people in a language other than English. My much improved conversational Spanish (I did have four years of the language in college but that was mostly grammar and literature as is customary) helped me feel secure on the trip, enabled me to communicate with and get to know people I would not otherwise have been able to interact fully with and has stood me in great stead on countless subsequent journeys. It inspired me to learn more languages in later years and afforded me the chance to do a kind of traveling I would otherwise have been unable to undertake. It helped make me a more independent traveler, a development which has enriched my life substantially. When we travel to Spanish lands, a rather extensive part of the world, I need neither a guide nor even much of a plan. We just go; we rent a car and travel.

Living there

After the cross-country trip, my desire to see the world grew continually stronger. The next important adventure I undertook, fortified by my Mexican sojourn, was to get the job working overseas that I referred to above. Three years later, at 25 years of age, I left to teach in Europe. (I did have a bit of hesitation about this undertaking since the Department of Defense asked on its application form if I preferred Italy, France or Germany as a location. Due to the nature of the war only some twelve years earlier, I was not anxious to go to Germany so I wrote my preferences as Italy, France and Germany in that order. Of course, I was slated for Germany. It was after all the Department of Defense). In order to take the assignment I had to put aside the prejudices I held both as an American and as a Jew. In doing so, I determined to approach people and the entire experience in as open-minded a way as I possibly could and make the most of my third choice. That was not easy but it was highly productive for my personal growth in many ways. After I arrived in Germany I was careful to make sure that anyone I was in the process of becoming involved with knew that I was Jewish. Until that time, I was not highly identified Jewishly, but my time in Germany had the anomalous result of making me more comfortable with and more interested in that aspect of myself. What followed were two years of footloose and fancy-free travel through a recovering Europe during which time I made several very dear, valued German friends with whom I passed many pleasant hours. Many of the young people of my generation were the children of Nazi parents, including at least one of my close friends. We did not talk a great deal about that but young Germans were frequently extremely interested in the fact that I was Jewish. That was quite understandable since quite a few of them had never met a Jewish person. Those circumstances forced me to examine what was most essential to me about being Jewish and what I wanted to convey to others about that.

At the close of classes on Friday afternoons, I would leave the North German town of Giessen where I worked and hit the trail, sometimes by myself, other times with another teacher, and driving to whatever place I could reach with a weekend at my disposal. It was not unusual for me to arrive back just in time for school's opening the following Monday. (Obviously, I did not mark too many student papers over the weekend.) During those two years as well as one that followed in Rome, I realized that the only way to really get to know a place comprehensively was to live there long enough to learn the language, make friends, and explore the area slowly and thoroughly. Of course, life does not present everyone with that opportunity nor do those who are so lucky always take advantage of the chance to live in another culture. Those three years were the only opportunities I had to live abroad although I did secure a job in Iran which was negated by my inability to take another year's leave from my place of work at the time. One of the things I found during my time working in Germany was that I enjoyed traveling by myself as well as with others. During those two years I was able to visit most of the interesting sites in Western Europe. I spent a full summer in Great Britain, several weeks in what was then Yugoslavia, and I made a couple of trips to Rome and Madrid as well as to the areas surrounding those cities. I journeyed all through West Germany, France, the Low Countries, Switzerland and Iberia. Only my inability to get a visa kept me from a summer in what was then Stalinist Russia. I had to wait another decade or so to visit that country.

The Perils and Rewards of Languages

As I got on the plane that carried me to Germany, in my hands was a Berlitz book on German; in my mind was a firm commitment that I would learn as much as I could right away and try to speak as little English as possible to any of the many English speaking Germans I knew I would encounter. I worked hard to keep that promise to myself in spite of some downright awkward and often embarrassing interactions. Soon after I got settled in my new surroundings, I began an intense study of the language with a competent English speaking young man I encountered on a visit to a German high school whom I hired as a tutor. My determination enabled me to master the language sufficiently well to pass as German[2] in normal conversations by the end of the second year. I even sat in on a course or two in philosophy at nearby, venerable Marburg University but I am afraid my reading and listening skills were not quite up to that challenge. Nonetheless, it was still rewarding to study in the 500 year old building and to realize that I understood about 75% of what was being discussed in a heavy academic area. I guess I needed at least another year of language practice to undertake that effort successfully. After lots of work and study as well as some really interesting miscommunications, I have enjoyed my relative fluency in German. What I did discover in the process was that the people I met were universally appreciative of my effort to speak their tongue. That has always stuck in my memory. The Germans I encountered during those two years would have been quite happy to practice their English skills with me, yet they felt respected by my resolve to speak German correctly and they were appreciative of the level of communication we were able to achieve because I had worked so hard. What I took away from that experience encouraged me to devote time and study to language from then on and, when I traveled to the Third World years later, even though I could not learn very much of a language in just a few weeks in a foreign land, I made sure I mastered at least the most common phrases for thanking or introducing myself to other people

---

2   In German one says the equivalent of "Is it warm to you?" rather than "Are you warm?" I learned that after mistakenly asking an attractive young woman I met on a train if she was hot. Unfortunately, we were within earshot of a then heartily guffawing crowd.

and for conducting simple purchasing and business transactions as well as other amenities and common phrases. In each instance, the positive responses displayed by those to whom I spoke were well worth the effort; however little I knew, my attempts at the simplest phrases helped to lessen the distance between me and people I met along my journeys and generated a multitude of smiles directed at me. The only problem with greeting folks in their own language is that, if you pronounce the words accurately (something I have a knack for), it is assumed you speak that tongue and the repartee is fast and comprehensive. If you choose to learn a few words and say them accurately, make sure that "I do not speak _____ (fill in the language)" is one expression you also master.

Upon my return to the States after being abroad for the two years in Germany, I had no more opportunities for further solo travel. I met my wife-to-be two months after my return from my first European trip and we were married the next year. She became my traveling companion everywhere I have gone ever since. Our travel was to exceed even my outsized determination and expectations.

The Kids Arrive

Not long after we were married, our kids arrived. However, that did not keep us waiting overly long to get started on our exploration of the world. Our daughter was but a year and a half old when we boarded a ship to Naples (third class of course) and our son was only six at the time. Nonetheless, I had taken a job teaching and consulting at the Overseas School of Rome. That took place during a sabbatical from my school in the outskirts of Philadelphia. The time in Italy became a unique experience for all of us. It was a totally new setting to which we all needed to respond and face challenges that we had never encountered before. From our small apartment in a complex which otherwise housed all Italian residents, Bev and I managed to journey each weekend to some accessible site of interest in the Italian landscape or to wander about in the marvelous city where we were living. Occasional stoppages of electric or water service in our apartment or driving through rather impossible traffic or standing in line for milk were but minor inconveniences. I think we might even have started pizza delivery service in Rome. We were not aware of any such arrangement at the time but there was a little restaurant about a block or so from our apartment whose pizza we liked a lot. I remember convincing them to send one to our apartment because the kids went to sleep early and it was so much more convenient for us that I did not mind paying a small delivery fee. The waiter would arrive to deliver the pizza in his restaurant attire and the pizza in the pan in which it had just been baked. I laugh even now when I think of that scene. Perhaps that was our great contribution to modern Italian culture. I am sure it is a very common and much more sophisticated process today. On free weekends we explored Rome as thoroughly as possible. We found that the saying, *Roma, non basta una vita* (a lifetime is insufficient for getting to know Rome) was absolutely true. We became adept at dragging two little kids all over the place, made friends with a few expats from other parts of the world and became accomplished Romans. And I learned Italian, again with stubbornness and perseverance and the help of a young tutor who lived a couple of floors below us in the apartment complex. Unfortunately, I had only one year for that endeavor which was simply not enough time for me to become as fluent in Italian as I had in German. Besides, I was working with Americans all day and was no longer traveling alone. My Italian just never reached the level I desired although I loved the sound of the language and made every effort to pronounce it like a true Roman. Bev was no linguist however and would casually say to our neighbors things like "Your hair looks lovely. Did you just come from the butchers?" or "I'll meet you later on in the tomato or in the cheese" confusing words like *pomeriggio* and *pomidoro* regularly. We have had many a laugh about those gaffes.

And so began my early adventures. I do want to note here that, although I use the word "adventure" frequently to describe my travel, I do not at all equate my experiences to the thrill-seeking undertakings that are often associated with the term. Rather "adventure" refers to my eagerness to experience the unknown, less traveled and more psychologically challenging pathways of travel. I am not an "adventure traveler" in the sense of the current use of that term; I do not seek high cliffs to ascend or wildly rushing waters to raft or other physical challenges to conquer. That is another kind of journey altogether, a style I respect but neither felt capable of achieving nor motivated to undertake. I am as likely to do a high bungee jump as I am to climb a skyscraper. Not if you paid me a million dollars.

But what did Germany and Italy and other European countries have to do with Third World travel? During the time I worked in those countries, there were Americans aplenty in Europe and our familiarity with the cultures of the continent was quite deep. A large percentage of immigrants to America had come from that area. We actually grew up in the thirties and forties with the notion that the history of the world was the history of Europe. Furthermore, technological development, clean water, sewage treatment, etc., were all much more like what we were familiar with in the United States then than those features were in less industrialized areas. That is the case, of course, even now. However, they were still dealing with the aftermath of the war. Small colorful villages which had changed little over the years abounded in Germany and France and other places. Fringe nations like Yugoslavia and Portugal which were more traditional and underdeveloped before the war began had progressed far less than Central Europe so their countryside harkened back to earlier times. There was also one additional overriding fact for the traveler. The dollar was mighty and travel was possible even on a relatively small American salary during the years I lived there. We made the most of that circumstance during our Italian year, though we did not get back to a recovered Europe again for a long time except for our summer trip through Scandinavia in 1971. That trip took us all the way to what was Leningrad at the time so there was even a short Second World interlude. And the technological differences between the U.S. and the Soviet Union at that time were very dramatic in spite of the general and possibly unjustified fear we had of their military might.

By the time our kids grew old enough for more extensive and productive travel for their personal growth, several more years passed and I had become the director of a camp for teenagers, thus locking in a series of summers without travel options. My financial ability to travel abroad was tenuous at best during the years our kids were growing up and our need for income to keep our household afloat was increasing. Getting away for long trips or having the money to take all four of us far away to the places I yearned to see became nearly impossible. Several times we were able to go to Mexico for short excursions with the kids during the winter school vacations. We explored Aztec and Mayan ruins together and enjoyed Mexican culture in a variety of places. Both kids were good travelers although my son was the more fascinated by it. It is he who has followed in my footsteps in his desire to dip his toes into the muddier waters of our world.

To the Third World

My transition to Third World travel was the product of several things but mostly my interest in cultures that were substantively different from ours. Mysterious India had always beckoned me although all of Asia seemed exotic and alluring, South and Central America became an extension of the fascination I found in Mexico, and, of course, Africa with its diversity, animals and traditional societies was another very appealing destination. And Europe had gotten quite expensive. I did not return there again after our 1971 Scandinavian trip until cruise lines induced me with their extravagant services and generous compensation in exchange for a few lectures I gave; they carried us free to some new places along the Mediterranean, Black and North Seas while they spoiled us with luxury at the same time. Those voyages eventually returned us to places we had visited earlier like Copenhagen and Barcelona and Venice. For the price, it was a great opportunity.

After a couple of such trips, Bev and I realized that this was not at all our style of travel. The free wine and delicious food and the easy packing and living were nice conveniences but the cruises were vacations, quite distinct from what we truly enjoy in our travel. A few hours, or even a full day in a port, offered a good opportunity to see architectural or artistic highlights or well known tourist sites which we enjoyed revisiting or exploring more fully but we got no feel for the people, had little time for leisure wandering, and had minimal opportunity to really sample the foods or music or other cultural facets of the places we visited. We could not pause at will or explore out of the way places or visit little villages. That aspect of our travel ended rather abruptly. What was economical and luxurious was just not fulfilling. Back to the road and on to the challenges of our more familiar style of travel.

As I noted above, our first winter vacation trips were primarily to Mexico. We were entranced by the various subcultures we found in that conveniently located and historically rich country and it has remained a favorite destination for us ever since we were a young couple with two small children. In a way, it has been a training ground for Third World travel for us beginning with the original trip I described earlier. We learned not to drink the water in such places. We wound up staying in lodgings where the electricity was intermittent and unreliable. We drove along roads that led nowhere and had apparently been maintained by nobody. We encountered countless people who lived on a few dollars a day or less. And, most importantly, we discovered that we could manage quite well without all the luxuries and accommodations we were used to at home. We have returned a score of times over a thirty five year period and still enjoy discovering new corners of the country. The fact that I speak Spanish helps us to be totally independent during our travels there. The freedom to do whatever you want, to arrive someplace and just take off wherever your inclination leads you makes for a promising trip every time. It was in the diverse subcultures of Mexico that I first became a mask collector and where Bev began to admire the folk necklaces she found in the street stalls and the stores. Mexico has sinced morphed into a popular beach escape for many Americans. We too have enjoyed days in Puerto Vallarta and Huatulco, Mazatlan and Zihuantenejo at the end of some of our trips, but we are not beach people so our time in those crowded, more expensive locales has consisted of a few quite limited, restful interludes from our exploration of the historical sites and archaeology of the country or from exhaustive pyramid climbing.

Challenges Galore

One of the true pleasures that I have discovered about Third World travel began with those early trips to Mexico. I came to delight in the increased creature comfort that I experienced after we returned home from our journeys, a sensation markedly reinforced by later trips to Africa, India, China, Central and South America, Burma, New Guinea

17

and Indonesia, etc. Accommodations in such places just do not customarily guarantee clean, flush toilets for guests. The quality of the water cannot be taken for granted unless one is thoughtlessly seeking to cultivate bacteria in his intestines. Transportation and roads are often undependable or non-existent. Food in restaurants or on the street is often unprotected by sanitation or refrigeration. Hotels are frequently substandard sometimes with uncovered pillows, old and tattered bed covers and blankets, and threadbare carpets. Showers, if they exist, are occasionally combined with toilet areas with a drain off to the side and no curtain. Hot water is sometimes a longed for luxury. Screens are exceptions in many places inviting flying guests to share the room. So why stay at such places? The fact is that they are often the only options available if the traveler wants to see things like the incredible funeral rituals of the Dogon people in the cliffs of Mali or visit a Spirit House in the jungles of New Guinea. And we do. Their economic benefits also help to stretch a trip a bit longer.

There is an additional bonus to the kind of travel I am describing here. We Americans, or at least very many of us, take a lot for granted. The fact is that there are about two billion people who live on $2.00 a day or less. Imagine that! Two dollars is less than a cup of coffee costs in a diner in the States. In the Third World I have encountered innumerable people who have no electricity and a majority in many places without plumbing, folks who draw water from a common well or carry it up hills to their hut from a nearby stream. I see one flimsy mud house after another with thatched roofs or tin shacks with no windows at all as we journey the Third World. Our first hand knowledge that people live that way in so many places sensitizes us to the reality of the experiences of so many others and enlightens us about our good fortune to be born and living in the industrialized world. I have come to appreciate deeply that our birthplace was merely a matter of luck, a hit on the human lottery, an existential stroke of good fortune. A survey of the possibilities brings to life the true meaning of the phrase: "There but for the grace of God, go I." Third World Travel would indeed be worth the effort for that insight alone.

When I tell people that India is my favorite place to travel, they often stare at me in disbelief. Their reaction is quite predictable. The typical response is something like "But what about the poverty? I could not take the poverty. And the dirt! Isn't it dirty there? And what do you eat?" Not only do such reactions indicate an absence of information about the country on the part of people who express those concerns, an understandable deficiency for folks who have never traveled to such places, but also a perspective on the world that can be both unrealistic and self-limiting. What does it mean when someone professes that they cannot deal with poverty? What does it say about what the world looks like to them and what does it imply about what responsible people should be doing about it? It surely cannot mean that one is unaware of the face of poverty, at least not in this time of modern communication. So we have to infer that poverty is just too ugly for some people to face directly. Once a reality is apprehended, perhaps there is something in an individual that makes him think it needs also to be addressed in some way, that it constitutes some personal burden or responsibility. Most folks surely don't want to go around intensely appreciating the suffering that exists in some other land (or perhaps a mile or so away in our own city) and acting as if it does not exist. As a matter of fact, poverty is usually just under our nose, right behind the wall that many of us build to protect us from the obligation we might incur if it connected to our lives. Could it be that it exists there in part because of that wall? I surmise that it is not poverty that keeps people from going to certain places but rather the palpable confrontation with the personal

19

implications of its realities that is so frightening. I remember a choice a philosophy professor posed to our college class. He asked if we would prefer to be "a contented cow or a disgruntled Socrates." Perhaps one's answer to that question determines in some way how we are to pursue our destiny and even how we are to choose our travel destinations.

I remember planning for a several week sojourn in India on our first long trip. Bev had a few commonly shared concerns about going to that country but she agreed to go for my sake. When it came time to organize our itinerary for the three month journey to Asia in 1987, we agreed to start in India so she could get that over with without worry for the rest of the trip. It did not work out that way for her at all. Had we never left India during that trip, she would have been quite satisfied. It immediately became a place of total fascination for both of us and remains so today. Our final stop on that journey was Japan, an interesting destination yet very well developed technologically and, for that reason, far less enchanting and different for us than the places we visited earlier in Asia. It was the country Bev originally felt she most wanted to visit but the opposite turned out to be the case. Of course, I should mention that we had been on the road for three months by the time we reached Japan, the dollar was weak against the yen and we could barely afford coffee with our meals; our stay there was unquestionably colored by these factors. We found and continue to find that one of the nice things about travel is how good it feels to get home and, by the last stop, we were also looking forward to reestablishing our normal lives in the comfort of our house and familiar surroundings. We were ready to just relax. I rarely think about any trip ending however. I try to stay in each moment of travel with every aspect of myself. They are valuable moments and I make an effort not to miss a single one of them. Mindfulness is a helpful companion on every journey.

Daily News

There are many rewards for the world traveler but personal enrichment surely holds a place at the head of the list. Every day I am reminded about that bonus when I gaze at the newspaper or watch a television broadcast about an area I have visited. The images in my mind about the locale which is the subject of the article brings a journey back to my consciousness and enhances greatly my ability to picture the people I met there providing me a palpable understanding of what that part of world is actually like. When a commentator talks about the mountains where the Taliban are hiding, I can picture vividly the Karakorum Highway[3] that we traveled on in Pakistan and the beautiful Swat Valley where so much violence has since occurred. I recall how we were directed not to go far off the road because there were no police or soldiers in that area. I remember the Pashtuns[4] that I saw in the villages along the way and how much I learned about the difficult life they lead in that secluded area. Even the road we drove on - highway or not - is actually impassable for much of the year. In my mind there still exist images of the mosques, the little stores we browsed through, and the modest hotel rooms we stayed in. It is often the case that a bit of news I hear

3 The Karakorum Highway is a road constructed by China and Pakistan to connect the two countries and was completed in1978 to encourage commerce between them. It carries vehicles during the non-snowbound months from near Rawalpindi, Pakistan over the Khunjerab Pass (4,800 m/16,000 ft) to Kashgar in China.

4 The Pashtuns are the same tribal group that has largely populated the terrorist movements in the area. They are speakers of Pashto and are the majority group in a varied, isolated tribal area that exists in the mountains of Northwest Pakistan and Eastern and Southern Afghanistan. They make up about half the Afghan population. They are mostly Sunni Muslims. The group has been the backbone of the Taliban in Afghanistan.

generates images and sensations that enable me to relive some of the excitement and tap into the knowledge I discovered in a particular place and that, in turn, enhances my sensitivity and understanding of the news itself. The Uyghurs we met in Xinjiang Province in Western China are now in open conflict with the central government and riots are taking place in many of the little streets we walked along in that area. The peaceful Monks of Burma that we observed praying and eating and walking along the roads have been brutally attacked and often imprisoned or murdered by the Junta that rules the country. The crisis in Honduras that was created after a coup displaced the president took place just a couple of years after our sojourn there. Obama's visit to Ghana followed the trail along the very coast where we explored. Reading about these events in the newspapers or seeing the pictures on TV not only helps us understand a situation that is being described but often enables us to identify more fully with the people who struggle in such places.

And there is the learning itself. What I have absorbed in school from my days in kindergarten to the defense of my doctoral dissertation was perhaps not as important or fulfilling or meaningful as that which I have come to understand through my travels and the reading I have done in relation to each trip. Perhaps that is because I was more mature in attending to the knowledge offered by my travel related discoveries, perhaps because my learning was more tangible, perhaps because of the deep interest I developed in language, culture, history, archaeology, geography, anthropology and other areas of study related to mankind's adaptation to settings and circumstance. As well as having gained much personal satisfaction in the process of expanding the scope of my understandings, I feel empowered by the acquisition of this knowledge. It helps me interpret important matters in my own life. It surely assists me in comprehending the current world in which I live. And if I get picked for a quiz show—who knows?

You are not Home Anymore

The differences between traveling in the West and exploring the Third World are quite distinct in many ways. Of course the people we meet in remote cultures look less like our neighbors and the buildings are often quite dissimilar to those we are accustomed to, as are such things as foods, shopping areas, transport, artifacts and pace of life, but there are more substantive differences as well which make travel in Third World locales quite an uncommon undertaking. The most noteworthy distinctions between the West and the lands we typically visit are those that have to do with values and beliefs – religious practices, observances of tradition, reverence for and treatment of ancestors, hospitality and the significance of guests, the level of regard for human life and expectations for a person's time on earth, the treatment of animals, the degree to which history is an integral part of daily living, and on and on. Each of these factors varies from place to place, of course. Bolivia is not Mongolia and Ghana is not Laos, but some of the values that are common in each place are correspondingly different from those of the more developed areas of the world.

Some examples of the variations in values and how they make travel more interesting illustrate what I mean about discrepancies between cultures. When people from the West think about parents and grandparents, we tend to do so with reasonable respect unless there is some special reason to feel otherwise. For most of us, the line extends backward to grandparents and even then only those whose lives have actually intersected with ours when we were young. We customarily take responsibility for such matters as funerals and burials for our parents. Our house may

23

include a number of pictures of ancestors, but we usually limit that to the preceding two generations except for notable relatives who have some historical connection to us and in whom we take pride. We sometimes relate stories about these people to our children or our friends, but that is about it. This is not the case in most places in the Third World. In some subcultures of Indonesia, for example, an ancestor is initially given a small burial and then the family saves as much money as possible to create a more elaborate ceremony some years later. Occasionally families are even known to bankrupt themselves in the process of funding the burial party. The second ceremony includes music, dance, an invitation to the entire village and relatives from islands far and wide, a reburial in some rather elaborate house-like mausoleum, and special prayers for the journey of the individual in the after-world. That is important because the ancestor then becomes an important spirit who watches over and assures well-being to the life of his or her descendants. Forebears become essences to be worshipped and appealed to for matters of personal welfare from that time on. This notion exists in some form in places from the Mayan area of Mexico and Central America to other American Indian cultures and throughout South Asia as well as in countless villages in Africa.

We have been welcomed at many such ceremonies in our travels and were treated as special guests who enhanced the import of the event by our attendance. If a mother or grandfather were being sent to the spirit world, the presence of apparently prestigious visitors from far away adds to the power of the ceremony itself and makes the voyage of the departed a more positive one. We are invited to dance at such observances, we are often seated at the front of the audience assembled for such rites and treated with special respect, and we are expected to participate as much as possible in the rituals. Such experiences cannot be duplicated in the West where one is more likely to be quite unaware that such events are even happening because, if they are, they are contained indoors and strangers are not invited. That is one of the important distinctions in the Third World travel experience. Many customs have their origin in and are deeply ingrained in the religious beliefs of the people and the underlying beliefs of a culture are quite often transmitted from generation to generation by stories and plays and puppet shows and songs. I have witnessed recitations of the great Hindu epics in shadow puppetry and in rich and colorful dances accompanied by the chanting of the sacred texts. I have watched magical ceremonies in spiritworshipping cultures where shamans work to cure illness or where the people invoke good harvests. I have seen vast libraries devoted to the teachings of the Buddha and the story of his life or those of some other important religious figure. People pray to statues of monks, to stones and effigies, to fires where incense smolders, and to other almost unimaginable objects. There is much more to say about values but these examples illustrate some of the kinds of opportunities that offered me a different level of adventure and serendipity and helped to satisfy my travel interests. Man has made many wondrous adaptations to life in this world. The enormous diversity in values that has developed from those creative changes is astonishing.

Some of the events and moments that have captivated me on journeys are spelled out in the following chapters and illustrate the deep experiences and many sources of personal growth that I attribute to my becoming who I am today. I know that even the act of writing this memoir is an exercise in tying together many disparate and consequential moments and making sense of the effort I have put into carving out this special niche in my world. I would unquestionably be a different person today had travel not become so central to me or had I been unwilling to make use of the opportunities I have had to pursue that interest.

CHAPTER TWO

WHAT DO YOU DO ABOUT THIS OR THAT?

"The sea is dangerous and its storms terrible, but these obstacles have Never been sufficient reason to remain ashore ... unlike the mediocre, intrepid spirits seek victory over those things that seem impossible ... it is with an iron will that they embark on the most daring of all endeavors ... to meet the shadowy future without fear and conquer the unknown."
—Ferdinand Magellan

Most of the people I know do not generally travel to the Third World. There are several likely reasons for their reluctance that I have been able to discern from conversations with my acquaintances and by the questions and comments I encounter from the audience during or after one of my lectures about The Third World. Without awareness of the possibilities inherent in Third World travel, there is little or no motivation to go to such unfamiliar places. When people are cognizant of the potential for excitement and personal growth in adventurous voyages and choose not to consider them (even after reading this book), it is quite likely that they have apprehension about some aspect or other, real or imagined, of off the beaten track travel. It is not just concern about exposure to the ugliness of poverty or the personal physical discomfort that might be encountered along the way that makes folks stop and think twice about such journeys. The unease is broader than that. My wife and I usually do not usually travel with others on our most challenging trips, but then many of our friends have very little desire to expend effort and spend money knowing they may be discomforted from time to time as they go along. Like most people, when they contemplate traveling from home during some leisure time interlude, they think more favorably of vacationing, perhaps with fantasies of sandy beaches, daiquiris and good service. An otherwise busy, hard-working weekly schedule understandably disposes many to seek escape and relaxation as opposed to challenge and exploration during their limited chances to get away from the daily grind. As I indicated, escape was not customarily my major desire even at the height of my work career but I too have spent time on beaches and I have indulged myself with good service and fancy quarters on a number of occasions. I have also occasionally gone traveling with friends but traveling with others has been the exception when I head to exotic places. To start with, when I go to Asia or Africa, I like to stay in those areas for three weeks or more which automatically rules out our friends who prefer not to be away that amount of time to start with or those whose work does not permit them to travel for such long interludes. The flights can be tedious, especially since security has become such a large part of the travel experience; it does not seem worthwhile to me to go so far for less than several weeks as it can often take a full day or more to arrive at a destination in Asia or Africa. We do not think folks take a pass on traveling with us because we are unpleasant travelers or especially controlling or irresponsible or late to dinner or loud in restaurants. (I could be wrong about this.) Actually, I assume that most of our friends just do not usually want to travel the way we do. We also sometimes prefer to be alone so we are not subject to the wishes of others. Traveling in a group is harmonious only when a spirit of compromise is present. We enjoy independent travel to places that lots of travelers consider a bit too unnerving or unstable or sometimes just plain scary to explore without the security of being with a group and under the management of some travel agency. Many people consider the organizing support group travel offers essential to their comfort and safety. I think such preferences are a product of folk's anxiety about going to places which do not guarantee creature comforts that are at least roughly equal to what they are used to having at home. Often the greatest component of their fear is concern about the possible lack of cleanliness and/or the threat of illness or infection that is assumed to result from less than our accustomed sanitary settings. This apprehension is especially typical of Americans for I encounter many Europeans, Australians and Asians traveling in places my compatriots do not seem to frequent. The second most articulated worry I hear people express is about food. "What is the food like there?" "Where do you eat?" "What do you eat?" As a matter of fact, I am not a person who eats just anything; I consider myself more persnickety than many of my friends, so I can relate to this concern. Although menu choices may be more limited and some foods unfamiliar, the fact is that hotels in the Third World have restaurants, and those places customarily offer enough potential food choices to keep even fussy travelers alive and healthy. One can always rely on such venues if there is apprehension about what might be offered at a home to which the traveler is invited or at some ceremony where unidentified or strange food is offered. Even the possibility of missing a meal now and then would not hold us back. I have missed quite a few in my travels as a matter of fact. The answer to "Where do you

29

eat when you go there?" is: restaurants, street stands with much care, hotels, places along the road, etc. I don't typically take peanut butter or snacks with me, although that is an accommodation one could easily make if food is a major worry, but I do occasionally pick up items in local stores and make do by snacking. Some kind of cheese or crackers or local edible fare is usually available in the equivalent of a grocery store along the road. That is a good idea when the journey is long and eateries few and questionable. We have never...really never...gone to bed starving although one mini-crisis did occur in this respect which I will share later on. On the few occasions when I have less to eat than I might otherwise desire, I keep in mind that most of the people we meet have not likely had more than one meal that day if they were lucky. That helps stave off panic. Actually, the less I eat, the bigger favor I feel I do for myself. I do not dismiss any of these concerns I have listed out of hand. It is all a matter of balance. There is no need to sacrifice comfort or develop new eating habits unless there is a payoff at least equal to the sacrifice. And that is the essence of my point; for me the payoffs far exceed the concerns.

Taking Care of our Bodies

Another question at the forefront of some of our friends' minds is "What do you do if you get sick?" That is a reality that needs to be dealt with, especially if the traveler has specific medical needs. We have been fortunate in being unrestricted in that respect during most of our travel, so my answer has usually been either a facetious-"There is a witch doctor or shaman just about everywhere we go, and they make house calls" (This is true, by the way) -- or more accurately and seriously- "We take basic medications with us and hope for the best." In fact the latter approach has served us quite well with a single exception and we were

30

lucky in that instance also. For the reader's convenience, I will offer a few suggestions for Third World travel in italics. Since this is not a *How To* book, I have limited that kind of specific advice to a minimum. *My travel kit includes a general antibiotic, aspirin, antibacterial cream, a hypodermic needle for certain areas, band aids, antihistamine, cold pills and lozenges. Over the past decade, I have also brought along antiseptic spray or wipes for cleaning my hands in places where the toiletry was wanting (and it usually is.)* I have used one or another of these items on quite a few occasions and did just fine. The fact is that there is usually some medical facility near most of the places we have visited even though the closest clinic or hospital may be less inviting than desired. *One can obtain a list of Western trained physicians in most of the cities in the Third World. One source of such information is an organization called IAMAT, the International Association for Medical Assistance for Travellers, which can be located on the web at http://www.iamat.org/.* I have spent many months in areas where I felt fortunate not to have to use the local facilities so I would not at all dismiss anyone's concerns about health and cleanliness. At the same time, if I did have to use local faculties, I am reasonably confident that I would have survived to tell about the event. My sense is that one needs to manage such fears by wise trip planning rather than allow them to become a rationale for avoiding the most exciting and challenging journeys that beckon us. The likelihood of getting ill and needing medical attention within any two or three week span of travel is relatively low for basically healthy tourists. Most such worries stem from anxiety, not probability. I can only recall two occasions in my travel experience (a remarkably low number) when physical issues needed attention and interfered with the quality or comfort of my trip.

Safety Issues

Safety is another bugaboo, one more pretext for cautious folks to confine their travel to the Caribbean Islands or Florida beaches or national parks. However, avoiding getting shot at or mugged or raped are matters to be taken into consideration in proper travel planning. This is especially true for women traveling alone. They are always more vulnerable to assault, robbery, and rape. *Where they can women should travel as often as possible in pairs.* Safety measures should be exercised in looking into a trip to a city where there is a high crime incidence or to a lonely countryside journey in the Third World. One often comes across articles in newspapers about the travails of American travelers abroad but the fact is that most such events closely resemble what happens here in the States on the streets of our cities or towns or in Europe or other relatively familiar places. Perhaps it is more comforting to imagine getting mugged in Atlanta rather than Istanbul but the results tend to be the same. Precautions help to ease one's anxiety and avoid disappointment or even physical jeopardy. We have had dangerous situations materialize which were palpably threatening and we even suffered a few direct hits, but more about that in a subsequent chapter. A few basic cautions are well advised. Of course, it is always good to check sources of information about current conditions in Kenya or Lima or Port Moresby if you are headed to other than the more commonly traveled places in the world. *One source which has information about such matters is the United States State Department's website at http:// travel.state.gov/ which updates such information regularly.* It is also important to remember, however, that the State Department's information tends to be pessimistic, overly detailed and even hysterical at times in its effort to be protective of American citizens, so one has to take the information with at least a grain of salt. *More accurate sources on the net include person to person sites such as www.Virtualtourist.com which enables the prospective traveler to communicate with people who live in the region he or she is considering going to or websites which feature reviews of travel destinations and facilities like www. tripadvisor.com.* More and more, such resources are available on the net these days. It seems like yesterday when information needed to be gleaned from books and brochures. Web sources keep expanding exponentially.

A clear photocopy of one's important papers, especially passports and traveler's documents should be kept separately during travel. That will make loss or theft much less damaging and can often serve in place of the documents for proof of identity to exchange money or transact some other business. *I have had wonderful success and peace-of-mind by wearing a money belt that looks exactly like a regular men's belt but has a zipper on the inside and holds as many as twenty or more bills.* That could enable me to take as much as a couple of thousand dollars with me in hundred dollar bills if I chose to do so. It also precludes a need to use bothersome traveler's checks or costly ATM's which are usually not readily available where I go anyhow. I have not used a traveler's check for about 20 years or more. *Using an ATM and most major credit cards adds a significant fee to a transaction.* So far I have yet to lose a single dollar from my magic belt. I always use the safe provided by some of the better hotels we stay in although most Third World hotels do not provide such luxury. These are just a couple of suggestions about how to keep disaster away, but tricks and precautions such as these are the kinds of things that keep one from having to impose artificial self-limits on itineraries and make whatever you decide to do more pleasurable and trouble free.

Watch Your Step

No matter how you prepare in advance, there is no question but that the Third World is more challenging than typical vacation travel. One of the real differences between adventuring through developing countries as opposed to vacationing in the midst of Western comfort and protection is the extent to which the people and the travel industry in each place concern themselves with the welfare of the traveler. In the Third World, one is just expected to take care of himself much more independently. With the possible exception of top level luxury group trips with guides and comprehensive controls, if you are in dangerous places and you fall, you fall. Climbing narrow, steep, steps on Mayan pyramids is up to you (although it has lately been banned at some sites to protect the monuments, not the visitors); ascending a cut-out log stepladder into the entrance of a longhouse in Borneo is the only way to get inside; stepping deftly onto an exposed plank over the water to board a sailing vessel in Halong Bay in Vietnam is the only way to get onto the ship you wish to board; crossing a deep crevice on a frayed, swaying rope bridge is likely the sole path to access the waterfall you want to see or the only entrance into the jungle village you want to visit (One wonders about the last time the rope was checked out by the local engineering department.) It is assumed you will meet the challenge but, if you don't, you either miss that place or worse. That is on the visitor. A lawsuit that solicits payment in Chinese yuans or New Guinea kinas for an accident or disaster is not a very promising undertaking. Safety just has a different meaning in the more remote places in the world. It is simply not a primary consideration for most activities to the extent that it is in the West. Just try to find a motor scooter or bicycle helmet in Kashgar or Hanoi or Managua. I dare you.

In fact, considerations about the availability of clean bed sheets and doctors, edible food and safe streets are all legitimate ones. At the same time, the places I go are frequented by many non-Americans who have not let such matters stop them from traversing locales where adventure and serendipity and uncertainty abound. I should mention here that Asian travelers do tend to go in organized groups however as do quite a few Europeans. Yet many foreign travelers seem to feel that out of the way places offer titillating opportunities rather than precarious and life-threatening undertakings. That makes me suspect that it is the traveler's background and reluctance to take risks that are more at issue in the "What do you do about....?" category than are the actual problems one is likely to encounter. There is that special moment when the Third World traveler says, "Phew! I made it!," a feeling that is quite remote from the perception of the beachgoer as he steps out of his chair, grabs his towel and makes his way to the luxury suite which awaits him. I personally have nothing against a clean and indulgent experience. I have sought that type of interlude from time to time as a welcome way to interrupt long, arduous travel in the backwaters of the world. If I can schedule one or more such stops along my way as a respite, I especially appreciate the opportunity. (I should point out, however, that some folks might not consider that my "luxury stops" meet their definition of what extravagance should consist of.) I especially recall my relief at arriving at a "real hotel" in Bhubaneshwar, India which had hot water, a nice restaurant and a few other Western amenities after a weeklong trip through dusty tribal villages in Orissa. Though I have stayed at some lovely places, such accommodations just do not offer me enough satisfaction to become the focus of the trip themselves.

Planning the Trip

I am frequently asked how I go about planning a trip. That is an important question because so much of the success of any undertaking depends on how one designs it. There is first of all the initial, overriding consideration of what country or region to explore that begins the process. For just about anyone I would imagine that is the major decision. Because I am so interested in travel, I read lots of related literature: history books, biographies of people around the world, travel articles and magazines (not usually the fancy magazines that advertise lots of cruises or specialize in beach locations or expensive hotels), and fiction by authors from many countries. The descriptions of Third World locations in such publications intrigue me and, at some point, I decide that I would like to explore a particular place or other. I then read about the country or region in greater detail in a guide book or I find internet articles or descriptions of travel there by others. I may also peruse suggested itineraries posted by travel agents. It is time for research. If my expectations are borne out, the place I have read about becomes my next destination and the details follow.

Another very good source of information has been the experiences of fellow Third World travelers. On my journeys I often have conversations with like-minded folks comparing our respective travel experiences and, I have sometimes made decisions to go to a place I would otherwise not have considered on the basis of what I learn from another traveler in passing. I recall, in this respect, a German family we met at a hotel where we were staying one night in a small town along the Silk Road in Xinjiang, Western China. They had been living in Beijing for several years because the man worked for a German company that had an office there. In the course our conversation, he mentioned that he had visited Sri Lanka during his time in Asia, not once but several times,. Although I was drawn to travel to that beautiful island (Sri Lanka was supposed to be one of the most appealing and interesting places one could explore), I had avoided going there because the civil war was quite active at that time. The newspapers were full of stories of bombings and other horrors of that conflict. He assuaged my uneasiness by describing the reality of travel there. It was just one year later that Bev and I journeyed to Sri Lanka for a reasonably safe and rich adventure we would otherwise have missed. We were not able (or even permitted) to travel to the area where the war raged, but most of the island was accessible to us and we had a great experience there. As it turned out, had we waited for the end of the Civil War, we would never have gotten to see the country. The war finally ended in May, 2009 by which time I would have been physically unable to manage that kind of trip.

Details about travel, even to lesser known destinations, are more accessible than ever now that the internet has become such an informative resource. It was harder to retrieve good, up to date information years ago when the traveler was limited to guidebooks or travel agent publications. These were usually quite sparse for Third World locations if they even existed; there were few guidebooks written about places most people never thought about going. Additionally, much of the information in guide books is already out of date by the time of publication. Now one can find how long it takes to get from village A to village B, what the roads are like, and what there is to see along the way practically anywhere people live just by connecting with someone who resides in that area or an agent who operates out of a city right in the country and who is personally familiar with the road. A few clicks of the mouse retrieve up to date flight options, hotel rates, and holiday and ceremony schedules. But you need to be willing to do a good bit of work to make it *your* trip. For me, that is well worth the effort although such is not the case for everyone. Most of the people I know who traverse similar paths either have fewer hours available or prefer to spend less time planning and take their chances that the trip will work out for them. That is a basic choice for all travelers of course but especially those headed for the Third World.

There is a middle ground however. I don't do it all. I usually follow up my research by creating a rough travel plan. A basic itinerary is not difficult to put together and it usually only requires a map of the desired locations as a resource. After I decide where I want to go, what I want to see and how long I want to be away, I customarily engage some folks on the internet who can give me information about the detailed choices I face. The sources are usually travel experts about the area to which I am going and they typically live in the region. Sometimes one can locate a very informed agent in the United States who has a lot of experience and really knows the destination area (most often an immigrant to this country), so that is frequently another option. Some years back, for example, we traveled to remote Dogon and Tuareg villages in Mali with www.Turtletours.com based in Arizona. We learned that the agency not only provides opportunities for charitable and helpful work with the tribal peoples to whom they are quite dedicated but also does a wonderful job setting up trips to the areas where the tribes live. Irma Turtle, the owner of the agency, has been to the locales for which she arranges travel on multiple occasions and is very involved with and solicitous of the people who reside there. There are quite a few other such caring people in the industry and the number seems to grow regularly. This is the process which I follow and which I recommend the reader try if he or she is so inclined. *When I feel I have gone pretty much as far as I wish to in my own planning, I then write a detailed description of our interests and needs, spell out which places I wish to visit and sketch out a tentative itinerary. I also describe our economic preferences as well as the level of comfort we desire on the trip. After that I go online to look at lists of agents and see how they present themselves in their advertising or I go to sites such as www.virtualtourist.com to contact knowledgeable people who live where we want to travel to gather their recommendations about places and agents. From the initial list of agents I have discovered, I then decide on five or so who appear to be folks I might possibly want to deal with and who are likely to understand our desires and needs. At that point, I send out an email with a rough sketch of the trip I want to take and I ask them to respond.*

The next step is up to the travel agents. My experience is that one can discern much from even their initial reply. Either the agent responds by showing he or she has an idea about what you want and has the flexibility and interest to work with you toward that end or you receive an answer which clearly eliminates them from consideration. A good example of the latter is a form response or a referral to a site which lists their options for group travel in the area you have written to them about even though you let them know that you prefer independent travel. That is the time to eliminate many of them from consideration. There is also a matter of fairness in communicating with agents you may not ultimately use to arrange your trip. Most travel professionals do not charge to work up an itinerary for you including making preliminary reservations, finding out details about what is available, or researching your questions. I rather quickly withdraw my request if we will not be going with them so that they do not do unnecessary work on my behalf. At the same time, I do continue to work with two or three agencies to refine the trip for some period of time since they are actually candidates to make our reservations. During the course of this process, it usually becomes clear whom I prefer. I then write the others thanking them for their help and explaining what I have decided to do. As I communicate with the final couple of agents whom I am still considering, I also let them know that I am in touch with another agency so everything is above board. They can decide how much of their time and energy they wish to spend on the possibility that I will ultimately engage their services.

But the planning is not at all over for me at this stage. Before our trip is set, I decide what we really need to reserve and what part of the trip I want to leave open, which items I want the selected agent to take care of and which I prefer to arrange directly, where I want a guide or a driver and where I want complete independence. These considerations, as well as the financial arrangements constitute an ongoing back and forth process. At the end, I have an itinerary, transportation, and several weeks that we look forward to. Depending on the area, the language, our available time and the circumstances, I leave as much of the trip open as I wish. The need to lock in reservations depends on how busy the time of year is, how available tourist facilities are, how much ahead of time I am planning and other such exigencies. *It should be noted here that direct reservations for hotel accommodations or transport can usually be cancelled rather close to the arrival date while travel agents usually require earlier cutoff times and harsher payment terms. This is good to remember especially if you have no travel insurance. As for insurance itself, my sense is that it is expensive and probably not worth the cost unless you have concerns about your health or other specific worries about being able to complete the trip.*

Packing

I am often consulted about how we pack for three week long journeys into parts of the world where many people tend to have about two days worth of clothing throughout most of their lives if they are lucky. The fact is that we probably do not dress all that much better than the residents anyhow. One of the main reasons for that is our wish to draw as little attention to ourselves as possible and to lessen the obvious differences between us and the people we visit in the Third World. There are plenty of other significant disparities between us and the folks we meet; every difference tends to increase the distance between the traveler and the indigenous people. Fancy or new or expensive dress is also an invitation to jealousy and even potential violence or robbery. Anything that lessens antagonism or even watchfulness on the part of the local people we encounter is an asset to the quality of our journey.

Over the years, Bev has become a world class expert packer. Somehow she is able to fit in the sparse clothing we start with and then add all the artifacts we collect along the way while still managing to close the suitcases by the time we head home. *We select about three day's worth of worn outer clothing, include an extra couple of pairs of undershorts and socks, and that is about it. We wash our clothing every night as we travel unless we are in motion or there is no opportunity or place to hang them to dry. If something doesn't dry completely we just put it in a plastic bag in the suitcase and hang it up in the next hotel. That leaves us with at least one full outfit on our back and one for emergency or special circumstances. The three day regimen has served us exceptionally well.* Should we lose or rip what we have packed, we have found few places in the world where there is no place to buy clothing necessary for travel. One can always purchase a T-shirt or a pair of socks at the local market even if they may not be of use after the trip. Prices tend to be much cheaper at those local markets than they are at home. That reminds me of one of the funniest travel experiences I ever had. We were in Nairobi, Kenya at the end of a safari trip during which our luggage was lost by the airline. As I describe later, we wound up having to buy a few cheap items of clothing in a local market. The clothes were poorly made and the material

41

was awful. We bought the items at the beginning of a three week trip and used them until our last day in Nairobi. At the market in that city, I decided to purchase a local carving which I liked very much. In the bargaining process, the salesman asked if we would like to trade any of our clothes for the carving. We had our bags along so I took out the Kenyan items which we had purchased earlier and offered them in trade. He eagerly grabbed them from me and handed over the carving. We were quite a distance away when he noticed that the labels indicated the clothes were made in Kenya: we heard him yelling that they were not worth the price. He had not asked for American clothes nor had we misrepresented in any way what we traded to him. The seasoned salesman just made a lousy deal and he was pretty annoyed. Of course, we will never know the actual value of the carving we bought either but we do enjoy it. He indicated his grandfather had done the carving. His grandfather must have been quite prolific because we saw the same figure several times over in our subsequent travels in Kenya. I think we wound up even.

For some years now, traveling by plane has been an increasingly arduous and sometimes painful experience. Taking all of your clothing in a carry-on or combining everything in one piece of luggage is a way of making the journey less stressful. That becomes increasingly the case as airlines began to charge for luggage. *The fewer articles of clothing you carry, the better.* Here I have to admit we are shoppers (usually for our grandchildren these days) and we do collect certain things (necklaces for Bev, masks for me, representative local artifacts for my programs) so *we take a folded up large soft, but strong, plastic bag that closes with a zipper inside our luggage. It takes up little space until we put all of our dirty clothing in it at the end of our trip and pack our more valuable and fragile purchases in the original suitcase we carried our clothes in.* That has worked out very well also.

Taking Control of the Trip

As I mentioned earlier, one option I have insisted on with very few exceptions is traveling independently unless we are on a trip with friends or someplace where one needs to join a group for some reason or other. At any rate, we want control of the journey- our itinerary, our time, housing, eating, visits and just about everything else- insofar as that is possible. It is more expensive to travel in a car or to have a private guide tag along in a city or even to employ a driver in the few places I dread to drive, but for us it makes all the difference in the world. I cannot stop a busload of fellow travelers to take a photo of people alongside the road. I cannot ask other folks to wait while Bev and I stroll leisurely through an interesting market or walk the back paths of some small village. I want to spend my moments in the way that interests me not at some compromised speed that is designed to accommodate the average interest and staying power of a busload of travel passengers. I also want to see the things I think are most important, I want to peruse my guidebook at a leisurely pace, and I surely want to spend whatever time it takes to communicate with the people I encounter. I like to get out of bed when I want to, even though I almost always want to have a very full day. Of late, I particularly want to rest a bit in the heat of the afternoon in tropical areas. I want to explore the town I am in during the evening and try out local restaurants and foods. One can rarely do these things without control over time and place. For me that is a must. Would I travel without the power to manage my trip? Only if I had to and then far more reluctantly and far less pleasurably.

There are other aspects of control that have been important to us in our travels, precious moments we would have lost doing it any other way. I remember vividly a trip in the heart of Sumatra when Bev and I were with a guide heading toward a wonderful village where the strangest of bullfights was taking place. I glanced at my guide book and saw that we were near a place I was anxious to visit, a jungle area where the Rafflesia[5], the largest flower in the world, grows. This giant, stemless bloom can be found only in a few places in Southernmost Asia and the Philippines. It can not only grow to a weight of over 22 pounds, but it is a parasitic plant that attracts insects with its foul smelling secretions. We were passing right by one of its rare habitats and I could not wait to see it. I casually asked our guide when we would come upon the Rafflesias and he offhandedly replied that we had passed the area many miles earlier. No way! My response to him was that we needed to turn back and I insisted strongly on doing so. Of course, such a discussion would have been quite impossible had other people been traveling with us, but they weren't. Our guide explained that he was not authorized to stop to see the flowers because they were not on our itinerary. I countered that he either needed to change the itinerary or call his office in Jakarta. When we got to a phone (pre-cell phone era), he reluctantly did the latter. I spoke with the agent and got permission for the guide to take us back. Needless to say, the guide was not happy with this change of plans or the extra couple of hours he needed to work that day but I would have forever regretted missing the opportunity to go into the Sumatran rainforest to see such a singular artifact of nature. As a matter of fact, when we arrived at the village that was at the edge of the Rafflesia jungle area, the guide asked if it was all right if he did not trek in with us. I was already displeased with him and happily found a couple of kids who took us into the rainforest to see the flowers we sought. We not only got to do what we wanted but we also enjoyed the youngsters who guided us,

---

5   The Rafflesia flower is named after Sir Stamford Raffles, the British Colonist who was known as the founder of Singapore. He led the expedition in 1818 that found the subspecies of the flower we visited.

met several of the village residents along the way and had a very enjoyable hike. It turned out to be a memorable experience. We also got to the next town in plenty of time to see our next highlight. the village bullfights.

Another example of an unplanned modified arrangement occurred on the island of Komodo east of Bali, Indonesia. At dinner a few days earlier on the Island of Sumbawa, we happened to be talking with a couple of fellow travelers who had been to Komodo and told them we were heading that way in a few days. They shared their experience on the island some time earlier when they stayed in one of the large, cabin-like buildings that stand at the edge of the forest near the coastline. It was important, they said, for us to know that those buildings were not only uncomfortable and unpleasant, but that there were both rats and bats in them and they were not desirable places to spend a night. I do not know if that is still the case since several years have passed, but their advice registered quite strongly with us. It turned out we were scheduled to stay in one of the "rest houses" so we explained to the captain of our small boat that we preferred to remain onboard instead and sleep overnight on the deck of the ship that brought us to the island. Since we already had a mattress and a blanket to rest on while we were sailing, we used them to avoid the various creatures we would have encountered there overnight. Our knowledge and control paid off once again. Such tips from travelers are commonplace in remote places and can be very helpful but, of course, only if they can be acted on. Becoming familiar with the area you are traveling in is very important also. Guides should not be expected to know or to pay attention to all the things the traveler might find interesting. A good example of this was our ride from Kashgar in Xinjiang, China toward Turpan at the other end of the province. Along the way, we saw the homes of some of several minority groups which reside in that area. They were varied in construction, the people were ethnically, linguistically and culturally different from one another and so they spiked our interest. We explained to our guide that we wanted her to stop at a home in each of these separate communities and inquire if we could visit. She was Han Chinese and was uncomfortable fulfilling our request but she did so in spite of her reluctance. There exists great animosity and resentment on the part of the Muslim citizens toward the Chinese government and toward the majority Han people especially. Nonetheless, we got to visit the Yurts of the nomadic Kyrghiz people as well as homes of Tajiks and Uyghurs along the way. It made the ride much more interesting and enabled us to meet folks we would not otherwise have visited.

As I mentioned above, we have had countless exchanges with other Third World wanderers which have enhanced our travel. We have heard from them about restaurants or foods to try, out of the way places to visit that do not show up in the guidebooks, interesting people to contact in the towns and villages, ceremonies to witness, hotel horrors and other pitfalls to be avoided, etc. These are all things that have the potential to make a trip meaningful and interesting and pleasant well beyond the written itinerary. I not only enjoy the conversations we have with the folks we meet but I am often humbled by how much braver and more extensive their itineraries are than mine. We do what we can but we are neither the most adventurous nor the most dedicated travelers on the road; some people we encounter amaze me with their tales of spirited undertakings. A couple from Belgium staying at the Hotel Kanaga where we lodged in the port town of Mopti, Mali told us they were leaving the next day to take the public boat that plies the Niger River from Bamako to Timbuktu. We knew the ship was so crowded that there was barely enough floor room for passengers to lie down, took three days for the trip, and included no restaurants or toilets. One needed to wait for the occasional stops in small ports along the way to purchase food or use the facilities. It sounded horrific and one could probably not have paid me to travel that way, but they were just doing the trip as part of their itinerary. That is the kind of courage I mean.

How complete our itinerary needs to be fashioned beforehand is also a variable in our planning. Because I speak Spanish and know there are ample facilities for visitors at the time I travel, I have no hesitation about flying into Merida, Mexico or Santiago, Chile and just finding a place to stay to begin a trip. We can easily arrange a car or other transportation when we get there and we need no guide to translate so our experience can be totally spontaneous. It is harder to do that in Vietnam or Sikkim or Togo where options are fewer and communication is limited. Independence and security go hand in hand as two aspects of a trip which the traveler must somehow balance in line with his style. Which consideration takes priority also depends on each particular location. All things being equal, I tend to favor independence,

So what else is there to worry about beside disease and sanitation, running out of gas or unavailability of medical care? Well, maybe rockslides and landslides, storms and floods, frozen roads and crazy drivers, marauding bandits and slippery thieves, insurrections and civil wars, spewing volcanoes and other such precarious hazards one might stumble upon. We have experienced some of these which I will recount in the coming pages. Frankly, I do not have any good advice for the reader about such things. Just try to avoid them if you can.

Onlookers at the Pushkar Camel Fair in Rajasthan, India

Fishing Boats on the lake at Ava, Burma

Mixed emotions in a little fishing village on the Island of
Lombok, Indonesia

Woman performing Mayan rites at the Church of San Tomas,
Chichicastenango, Guatemala

CHAPTER THREE:

HIGHLIGHTS

"One of the gladdest moments of human life, methinks, is the departure upon a distant journey into unknown lands. Shaking off with one mighty effort the fetters of habit, the leaden weight of routine, the cloak of many cares and the slavery of home, man feels once more happy."

— Sir Richard Burton

Our travel has produced many very special, exhilarating moments as well as some conspicuous low points all interspersed with a multitude of varied experiences in between. Peaks and valleys inevitably occur in travel as they do in daily life and the hope is that the memorable moments that happen will compensate for the hardships, disappointment or failures one endures along the way. But there is no guarantee that everything balances out at the end; travel, like our existence in general, requires a dose of optimism, a bit of luck, good planning and common sense to make an overall positive experience possible. One is more likely to encounter life-changing experiences roaming through the Third World; what happens on those far away journeys can modify the traveler's very outlook on life or his understanding of himself or the world around him. These are the true potentials of such adventures. It is the singular moments of such travel that really count.

Down the Ghats

For me there were times when I entered into a veritable state of awe as I stood beside events or gazed upon places that almost overwhelmed my senses. It is hard to know what the ultimate effects of such experiences are, but one recognizes these moments when they occur if we are open to them. Words fail, the soul feels moved, the senses quicken and the moment itself is frozen in time. One such experience captured me on a magical morning in the city of Varanasi in India, an ancient center of Hindu civilization that is as full of mystery and spirituality as any place I have ever traveled. I remember the day my wife and I awoke in our modest hotel on a hill high in the city. It was barely dawn. There was just enough light to see mosquitoes diving into the glass door that separated our room from the small garden outside. We dressed, set out without eating and met our guide at the entranceway to the hotel. We strode briskly down the hill toward the River Ganges, alongside a few other souls awake at that unlikely hour who were also descending the same path. It was already getting warm outside even though the sun had not yet risen.

We made our way down the large steps or *Ghats*[6] that led to small rowboats tied below at the shore of the river and climbed into one of them along with our guide. The water was tranquil and the Ghats were rather empty except for a few folks camped along the hillside underneath the ancient, abandoned hotels that loomed above them. It was yet quiet enough to hear the calm water lapping gently against the side of our boat. As we headed out toward the

---

6   The large steps which lead down toward the Ganges River in Varanasi are called Ghats. They have cosmic significance for Hindu believers which fits with their concept of divinity.

deeper area of the river, our guide lit a candle which he had affixed to a small, floatable tin platform and placed it into the water. This was a common religious ritual and we were to see a number of such candles floating alongside our boat as we paddled along. And then the sun finally began to pierce the darkness. The following half hour or so is deeply etched into my memory. As the sun slowly illuminated the scene, we witnessed hundreds of Hindu devotees descending the paths leading to the river. They gathered together all along the riverside and methodically immersed their bodies into the water performing ageless rituals to purify themselves in the holy Ganges. It was a panoramic dance of devotion. The edge of the river and the Ghats themselves were eventually packed with what appeared to be thousands of pilgrims and worshippers fulfilling their respective dreams culminating in what we came to understand was a lifelong aspiration. I have never witnessed a more devout setting than the one I viewed at Varanasi that morning. We watched cremation fires start alongside the river as tradition has dictated for as long as anyone remembers; the power of the people's beliefs was almost palpable in the air and fixated my attention on every detail. I was truly enraptured. If I had no other experiences in India except for observing that one ceremony that morning, the moment would possibly have justified the entire voyage in my mind. We returned several times to India afterward and the country has since become our favorite destination. India seems to offer a wonder a day. There are amazing ceremonies that take place all over the country throughout the year. Varanasi was only one of the miracles we discovered there.

Pancho and Us

Awe-inspiring experiences are, of course, not at all limited to India. A few years later, we had an equivalent happening occur on a trip to Peru. We found the colorful country captivating throughout our entire trip, but again one particular moment remains unforgettable, a product of unusual serendipity. We had originally planned to spend a day whitewater rafting on the Urubamba River, a scenic waterway that runs through the mountains east of Cuzco. As I mentioned before, one gets the best information from like-minded travelers, one of whom we encountered in our hotel in Lima near the start of our visit. As we compared our respective plans, I learned from our fellow traveler that the water in the Urubamba was quite cold at that time of the year. My past whitewater trips had taught me that one gets soaked to the skin even without falling out of the boat which is also a likely occurrence. We decided to skip the river after that conversation and found ourselves with an extra day. We had also learned earlier from someone else that there was a small hotel at the top of the mountain right by the Machu Picchu archaeological site. It was recommended that we stay there if the opportunity presented itself so we traded the Urubamba for a night at that lodge. Good decision.

The day-tourists arrive at Machu Picchu sometime in the late morning and they leave about 2:00 or 3:00 pm after touring the dramatic site with its old terraced farming areas and its multitude of mysterious buildings and paths. During that time, it is an interesting place to explore, but when the others leave, the few who stay at the hotel have the place all to themselves, very much like being in a museum after hours. We had the chance to be at the site virtually alone the remainder of that day and we took advantage of that. No one else from the hotel wandered back to the site after the buses and the crowds left. But Bev and I and one of our friends strolled back into the heart of the old site and, except for one guard and Pancho, the llama who lives there, we were by ourselves on top of the Andean world. We had met Pancho earlier in the day and we knew enough to bring some bread to make friends with him. We strolled the same paths as we had in the morning, imagining the sounds and spectacles that must have existed there five hundred years earlier. As we sat on the ancient stone steps to rest, the sun was descending and, wonder of wonders, large, billowy clouds began to roll into the valley below. Soon, the hilltops underneath us were covered and we became virtually surrounded by the cloud cover. We stood there in amazement as the entire mountainside slowly disappeared in a cottony haze. The Inca who lived there must have witnessed such moments many days of their lives. The buildings began to disappear until we felt like we were floating at the top of the world thanks to the conjunction of the forces of nature and the uniqueness of the history of this special place. The paths, the terraces, the buildings, the llama, the surrounding mountains and we ourselves were all soon enveloped together as if one. If I have ever had a more magical moment, I cannot recall it. It was not only the highlight of our entire Peru trip but it is a picture that remains deeply engrained in my memory. It was a fitting conclusion to that part of our trip after a delightful, picturesque train ride took us to the long hidden site and a motor coach ascended the twisting road to the top of the peak while a youngster ran straight up the mountainside racing us to our destination. What a wonderful place!

At the Dig

It was early in our Third World travels when we went to China for the first time. One of our special experiences occurred in the city of Xian. It is in that ancient capital that the famous terra cotta soldiers of the Qin Dynasty still stand guard to protect the emperor in his afterlife. Those hundreds and hundreds of artfully carved warriors (it is estimated that there were about 8,000 such figures originally), each one distinctly modeled after an actual soldier in the royal army of the time, constitute one of the most popular travel destinations of the world. We were aware that this site was already a popular place to visit and that we shared this experience with many others but witnessing the location was something special. When we visited many years ago, the dig was well underway but far from complete. I no longer remember how many archers, horses and horsemen, and spear carriers had been excavated by that time but I can still picture many hundreds of life-sized figures arranged neatly in their respective marching positions. Only the ropes which once connected the riders to their horses and the wooden spears they brought to their afterlife battles were missing, decayed and lost after having been placed in their hands two millennia ago. But the dig was still very much in process. We were to visit other active excavations in our travels, yet this was overwhelming even though it was quite incomplete and we felt as though we were viewing a treasure emerging from beneath the earth. Each man's face was different from the next, each position was lifelike and the careful unearthing of history was taking place beneath a gigantic tent in the middle of a field. It was different from Machu Picchu or Varanasi, but the experience of actually being there and viewing this amazing site while it was relatively early in its development, of imagining the existence of a culture which would create such a military force for the afterworld, while we were traversing a still mysterious and relatively untouristed China at the time, was, again, one of those travel moments that makes all the effort worthwhile. We walked through the entranceway into the open dig which seemed virtually unguarded and felt much like we had discovered the mystical army ourselves.

The Poor Pigs

The Indonesian island of Sulawesi (formerly known as Celebes, thanks to the headlines of World War II) was the site of still another incredible travel moment for me. My experience was indicative of the very best and most astounding things one can stumble across in the Third World. We went to visit a village in the center of the island where the Toraja tribal people live because we had read about their unusual and very interesting funeral rites. We were not sure initially if we would find a funeral ceremony in the rice field and canyon covered heart of this fascinating island but we were fortunate enough to get to see one in progress. It was one of the most unique and fascinating events we had ever viewed. We approached the town where the ceremony was transpiring by passing through a valley where wooden effigies of the dead stared down upon us. They were all dressed up and propped against fences at the opening of caves which towered as much as forty to fifty feet high on steep sides of hills. These were creations commissioned by local families to honor their dead and to position them for an afterlife of featured viewing of the beautiful fields below. But that was just the beginning. As we neared the village, we began to see other people moving along the paths toward our common destination. We joined the trek and arrived at an encampment in an otherwise undisturbed forested area. We saw literally hundreds of people there most of whom were seated inside large tents. We learned that one of the tents was for close relatives, another for the immediate family and several others for friends, neighbors and visitors who wanted to be there. All were welcome. There was food and drink for everyone the way you might find at a festival or wedding in that part of the world. The honor of the dead person was apparently enhanced by the many guests that came for this ceremony. The saying, "The more the merrier," surely applied in this instance. We were directed into a tent where we sat down and partook of the generous food offerings. Family and friends of the deceased served us graciously in our tent.

While my wife sat on the cloth spread on the ground for

her comfort, I followed the sound of a pig screeching a few yards away and saw before me an unfortunate animal trussed up and tied hanging upside down from a pole as it was being carried into an open area by two men. The pig seemed to be keenly aware of the part he played in this pageant because his distress was quite evident. His comfort was also quite questionable. My wife was equally aware of what was to happen and she declined to join me at the site. The men laid the pig onto the ground on its side, took out a long knife and plunged it into the animal's heart. It was far from an instant death however. The pig screamed in desperate pain and wretched back and forth for many minutes before succumbing. As if that were not appalling enough, while the animal thrashed about, one of the men pressed his fist tightly over the hole created by the lethal blade to hold in the blood and capture the moisture inside the soon to be roasted carcass. After the pig died, it was skinned and cleaned in short time and carried to the cooking area destined to serve the glory of the deceased and the appetites of the guests. While all this was transpiring, the effigy of the dead person in whose honor the ceremony transpired and for whom the pig gave his life looked on from an adjacent tent. Meanwhile folks prayed over the actual coffin that contained the corpse of the deceased which had been originally buried some two years or so earlier. This second, festive burial we were attending was held so that all who could come would be able to arrange to travel to the ceremony, even from distant islands where they may have emigrated during their lives, and so that the family itself could save enough money to sponsor the event. We were informed that this was the ideal, traditional way for the Toraja, especially those with sufficient means, to fully provide for the deceased's stay in the afterworld. Wealthy families even imported skilled Balinese carvers from that nearby island to make the effigies as lifelike as possible. It takes a very powerful belief to create so elaborate and expensive a ceremony. We learned that some families have gone into the equivalent of bankruptcy after arranging too elaborate a ceremony and leaving little to support the living relatives of the deceased. Again, we had a view into another extraordinary and mystical part of the world we inhabit.

Before we left Sulawesi, we had to drive back to Ujung Padang where we had first arrived from Bali, Shortly before we reached that port city, we noted another ceremony in a building along the side of the road we were driving on. There was a fairly open front to the building and we could see that there was a crowd of folks inside, a band and some kind of celebration. Again, we decided to investigate. Our guide inquired about the goings on and returned to our car to tell us that there was a Makassar[7] Muslim wedding going on and the people had invited us to join them as guests. What a scene! There was one of the most unusual rock bands I have ever witnessed playing unfamiliar and loud music, there were tables full of food and various sweets, and the bride and groom sat at the front of the room dressed like a king and queen. They welcomed us, invited us to stay as long as we wished and asked us to partake of the feast. We had one more wonderful taste of a different culture and experienced another instance of the hospitality of the area. We parted from Sulawesi full of the experience and ecstatic that we decided to visit the island.

A Monkey on his Back

All travel highlights are not necessarily awe inspiring however. Some are just unforgettably amusing or

7   Makassar is the capital of the south province and the largest city on Sulawesi Island. From 1971 to 1999 (we visited at the end of this period of time), the city was called Ujung Pandang, after a pre-colonial fort in the city, The two names are often used interchangeably

entertaining or informative or even just challenging. To qualify as a highlight, I would say that an event does have to be memorable at the least. Given that criterion, one occasion I will never forget occurred in the town of Iquitos, a Peruvian gateway to the Amazon Rainforest. We spent a day or so in the rustic riverside village before we were to embark on an Amazonian boat ride. Friends who were with us and Bev and I decided to visit the little zoo that was a couple of miles out of town. We had gathered from other travelers that it was an unusual place to visit—and that turned out to be an understatement. To get there we rented two small mopeds and drove ourselves to the site. The most unique thing about the zoo was that many of the animals were roaming about within reach of the visitors and vice-versa, especially an assortment of monkeys. As a matter of fact, just as we entered the site, one of the free ranging monkeys jumped onto the back of my friend, Ben, put its arms around his neck and stayed there throughout our entire time at the zoo. I know it was not the most comfortable experience my friend ever had, but for the other three of us it was hilarious. Every time we looked over at Ben, we laughed. The monkey could not have settled in more comfortably on its new beast of burden and the photo ops were wonderful. If I still cannot forget that adventure, I know Ben surely carries it even more vividly in his memory. As if that were not insulting enough for our group, at another point one of the other monkeys ran by and somehow snatched the keys to one of our mopeds. It would have been a long, hot walk back without our buggy so we spent quite a bit of time cajoling that animal. We did not get those keys back until we had worked on the problem for over an hour. Eventually our adversary got bored teasing us and dropped them near us from a tree branch. Among the other treats of that day, an attendant who was holding a gigantic constrictor from the jungle offered us the chance to do the same. I accepted the challenge and took the massive snake from him holding it as far from my body as I possibly could. There are few opportunities to be so intimate with such powerful animals. I was glad I tried it and equally glad the moment passed without untoward consequences. The overall experience was unquestionably my most eventful zoo visit ever. It was yet another instance of complete serendipity that occurred touched with both humor and remembrance.

Exploring with Kids

I imagine one can also label an episode a highlight when plans work out so well that the result surpasses even the most optimistic expectations for a trip or an event. Four such happenings occurred to me in recent years. Those were journeys with my family – my two children, my son-in law, daughter-in-law and five grandchildren- to Nicaragua, Guatemala, Panama and South Africa respectively. We haven't been in a position to do that kind of thing until very recently, primarily for economic reasons, but additionally because the grandchildren were too young to appreciate the kind of travel we prefer. We discovered how extraordinary an undertaking it can be for a family to experience the Third World together and to jointly meet whatever challenges present themselves along the way. Of course, for these voyages, the focus was mainly on the kids and their enjoyment. Bev and I had been to all but one of those places earlier. The family journeys provided surprises and unexpected highlights that will remain with all of us forever but especially with my grandchildren. One does not need a cruise ship or a resort to bring the family together and provide a bonding experience.

Bev and I had not been to Nicaragua before and we did not know what to expect there although we assured our gang that they would have a good time. The parents were nervous and the kids were a little skeptical. We anticipated such would be the case so we communicated the optimism and confidence that have always characterized our travel to the two younger generations. They had their doubts (mostly medical or safety issues for the younger kids, like many Third World travelers) but my past trips to Meso-America gave me assurance that a trip to that area would be worthwhile and interesting. And we did find excitement. We climbed paths to the top of accessible volcanoes where smoke rose steadily from inside deep craters. We rode a zip line that hurled us from tree to tree through the jungle. We spent time on deserted and beautiful Pacific beaches. We were even guided by a native Nicaraguan to one lovely, isolated seaside spot where the kids were able to participate in the release of tiny sea turtles from a sanctuary. They helped put those little creatures onto the sand and watched hem wind their way into the water some 50 feet or more from where they were placed. They could barely contain their delight at the opportunity and they could hardly wait for our return to the States to share the experience with their friends and schoolmates. That was surely a highlight for them. Witnessing their joy was a highlight for us.

Guatemala is a bit more attuned to tourism so we had less time to just roam around alone and fewer uncertainties to deal with. But the ending to our trip was a stay at one of the most comfortable and enjoyable kids' places we could have found anywhere, a complex of lovely hotels sandwiched between an amusement park and a water park all located near the small town of Retalhuleu, a three hour drive west of Guatemala City. The recreational area belongs to a workers' organization called IRTRA which is a facility created by the government so that Guatemalan workers can enjoy a Disneyworld-like vacation with their family for a very affordable rate in that mostly poor country.

Visitors from abroad are permitted to stay at the resort and enjoy the recreational opportunities also although they have to pay about three times as much as Guatemalans do for everything- not an overly burdensome rate considering the value of the dollar there. The place is officially known as Los Hostales de IRTRA. From a beautiful, well kept and still extremely inexpensive hotel area a little open train takes vacationers to the equally economical amusement park and the thrilling water park just outside the hotel area. It was Disney-like indeed, except for the absence of long lines, the manageable dimensions of the park, the absence of other American tourists and the affordable prices. With their entrance ticket for either of the recreational parks the kids went on whatever amusements they wanted to as often as they liked and they definitely got their money's worth going from ride to ride until their legs gave way. No complaints were heard about that trip either. A subsequent trip to Panama offered equal delights for all. Among those were visits to traditional Indian villages we accessed in a dugout canoe where we ate food prepared for us served in banana leaves. We also had an informative viewing of the Canal and visits to several natural sites including an island full of monkeys. Years later, these voyages are constantly referred to as wonderful times by my grandchildren, so I guess that qualifies them as travel highlights. The fourth trip which took us all to South Africa and on safari near Kruger Park, villages in Swaziland and historical sites of recent history such as Soweto and Robbens Island where Mandela was imprisoned was remarkable and will constitute eternal memories for all of us. More about this later.

Festivals, Parades and the Cure in the Field

While some highlights of travel can be the result of careful planning; others just happen. Knowledge of the existence of a special event that occurs regularly is a good basis for developing an itinerary which includes a chance to see people doing something that they plan for each year- a parade or carnival, a religious event, a wedding or other life event, a special celebration, etc. *For anyone intending to visit the Third World, I strongly recommend researching that kind of potential occurrence to enhance the likelihood of seeing people dancing, dressing up, courting, praying or performing any other life activities.* We have been to some dandy festivals in our travels. These happenings usually feature crowds of people, lots of activity, and memorable, often ageless, folk customs. The Periheras of Sri Lanka, the Bhagoria Festival of the Bhil People in Madhya Pradesh, a very isolated tribal area of India, the Day of the Dead celebrations in Mexico, the Camel Fair in Pushkar, Rajasthan, Carnival in Salvador or Rio in Brazil, celebrations of historical events, major religious ceremonies, large fairs and other similar activities afford the traveler a peek into the lives of the celebrants and the essence of the cultures in which they live.

Madhya Pradesh is a dry, farming section of India north of Mumbai. There are several tribal peoples that occupy the area, primarily the Bhil and the Bhilala. We went there to visit their societies and chose to do so at the time of the year when their most important social event takes place although we needed to endure the uncomfortably warm weather that prevails at that time. Bhagoria means "running away" in the local language and the festival we attended gets its name from the courtship customs that occur during the festivities. The villages are a good distance from one another in this section of Madhya Pradesh so encounters with other large groups of one's fellow tribal members have to be organized. This is achieved by arranging several amazing get-togethers which involve thousands of people who live many, many miles apart. These parties occur in a few local market towns over a period of about two weeks, some lasting a single day and others a several day period.

Folks arrive early in the morning for the festivals, dressed in traditional, home-made outfits of a color they have arbitrarily decided upon in their respective village; they arrive carrying musical instruments and ready to party. It is time for the boys (sometime also men who are not completely satisfied in their marriage) to meet young girls from other villages. The boys play their decorated, home-made flutes and drums and they and the girls dance facing one another in concentric circles to interact with and get a good look at potential mates. If a flirtation becomes serious, a boy invites a girl to run away with him into the woods where they will stay together for a couple of days to try out their partnership. If all goes well (I leave the readers to apply their own imagination to that concept), the girl is invited to the boy's house and his parents negotiate a marriage arrangement which includes an acceptable bride price (a complete reversal of the Hindu customs followed in the surrounding majority culture.) The colors of the self-made dress of the young people who attend the event are bright and dazzling. The energy of the entire festival is so elevated that people seem to dance above the dusty ground as they move along. Visitors are invited to join in the festivities though I do not know what the reaction would be if an American tried to drag one of the girls off into the woods. I suspect that might not be the popular thing to do. At any rate, I did not have the opportunity or the inclination to investigate. Bev and I do travel together.

In the midst of the Bhagoria festivals, there are literally thousands of people moving from one dance circle to the next. There are lines of young men playing flutes marching through the crowd. The area is rimmed by amusements like non-motorized Ferris wheels for the youth while vendors sell every kind of local food including special sweets that show up only during the Bhagoria cycle. There are no permanent tourist facilities in any of these villages but staying in a tent on a Maharajah's open field was more than worth the experience. It would be hard to arrange to be in the midst of this festivity independently so, in spite of our preference for traveling alone, we were with a small group of fellow travelers. We didn't even mind that, an indication of how exciting this experience was.

The Camel Fair

Another highlight festival we attended in India is considered by some to be the most spectacular in Asia. I cannot evaluate that claim except to say that we spent several days in the city of Pushkar in Rajasthan at a time when there were more camels and more pilgrims present than two such groups intersect anywhere else in the world. This Camel Festival is an occasion when camel and horse owners assemble to trade and sell and buy these animals, some of which are all gussied up for competitions which are central events at the fair. I never imagined that camels could be trained to do the tricks we observed in the large sports stadium where the shows took place. On one side of the stadium are the large fields with hundreds and hundreds of animals and their owners who seem to spend the day shaving and decorating their respective treasures while the camels sit there undergoing this special attention and complaining constantly. The tents extend more than a mile around.

A relatively short walk from the fields is a small lake in the center of town alongside which stands a temple dedicated to Brahma, the Hindu god of creation whose wife cursed him by denying him his share of temples on earth. Pushkar was the exception she allowed, however, and there were thousands of pilgrims in town to celebrate Brahma's settling in this town and by this lake to make the area his holy spot on earth. As was the case in Varanasi, pilgrims came to the lakeside from dawn to dusk to purify themselves in the holy water and to make their prayers to the god they worship. The splash of colors and activities could only take place in India. At one location or other children can be seen doing circus acts, the streets are teeming with peddlers and tourists and pilgrims, the colors of clothing and cloths are infinitely varied and bright, the smell of foods (vegetarian only, no meat is ever allowed into the holy city) and incense fill the air and one shop after another beckons the collector. A highlight—you bet your life!

Blood in the Street

One other special day of my travels was a unique event that is part of the Muslim calendar and was being celebrated quite dramatically in Egypt during the time I was visiting the country. I was unaware of the existence of this unusual occurrence until we went out onto the streets in the morning with the guide we had engaged. It would have been difficult to miss the happenings that took place on Eid al Adha, a Muslim holiday during which folks who can afford the cost commission the slaughtering of one or more animals as a fulfillment of an obligation spelled out in the Koran. The meat of the animal is then divided and at least one third of it is given to poor families. On this day butchers stand in front of their shops throughout Cairo and other cities and systematically kill domestic animals dividing and distributing the flesh. Almost everywhere one can see lambs or cows or goats, freshly slaughtered, lying on the sidewalks in pools of blood or hanging on hooks outside the butcher shops while the owners and their helpers carve them into manageable pieces. Around each of these scenes stand representatives of the recipient families awaiting their share of the donation. Interestingly enough, my guide asked that I explain any photos that I took for my audiences fully and sympathetically. He was afraid I would disparage the practice of the day and that people would infer that Egyptians were barbaric rather than observing a religiously mandated, traditional holiday of generosity. I assured him that I would make sure that all who viewed the images I carried back would receive a full description of the charitable roots of the process they were witnessing.

Indian Delights

Every day in India may not be a travel feature but it is the most likely place you will wake up to one. I mentioned the Bhil people and their Bhagoria Festival above but there are over 40,000,000 minority people in the country, many of whom live outside the surrounding Hindu culture in respect to tradition, history, language, religion, ethnic background or some combination of these societal attributes. The Bhil are the most populous group of the tribals numbering some 6,000,000 alone. Traveling well off the beaten track is the only way to meet these groups because those who have substantially retained their cultures have done so by staying out of the cities and interacting as little as possible in mainstream socializing and commerce. One day in the very rural area of Orissa in the East we rode along a road in the neighborhood of the Kutia Kondh tribal group. As we drove, we spotted a group of women sitting in the corner of a field just off the road. We could not tell exactly what they were doing until we parked and walked closer to them. Their focus was intensely directed toward their activity so it was as if we were not even in their presence. As a matter of fact, I was ignored by them the entire time I watched the ceremony making it possible to take sequential photos of what was going on without intruding on the serious business before me. It was rather clear we were welcome yet we barely exchanged looks and nothing was said except for a few words between one of them and our guide to ensure we had their permission to be there.

The activity the women were engaged in turned out to

be a shamanistic cure for a sick youngster about ten years old. I do not know what his illness was but the process itself was quite incredible. They did not seem to mind my recording on camera each of the steps they took to take away the child's apparent fever. The shaman, or leader of the group, first led the preparations for the ceremony by directing the other women to prepare a pot of water, which she followed by drinking some other liquid from a bottle herself, chanting and seemingly putting herself into a trance state. As that was developing, after about a half hour or so the child came out of the nearby woods wrapped in a white cloth accompanied by his mother. Each of them carried a live bird by the legs, the boy a pigeon and the mother a chicken. When they reached the circle of four women, they handed over the birds which turned out to be essential to the curative process. The four women began to feed rice to the birds so that they would be full and satisfied before being used to take away the disease the boy was suffering from. The pigeon did not seem especially hungry but that dumb chicken pecked away as if it were at a party. At one point, the boy was held still while rice was placed on his bare stomach, then on his hair and finally upon his lips which the chicken enjoyed as it cleaned each area in turn.

After another half hour or so, a man carrying a little bow and several arrows appeared along the same path from which the boy had come; we assumed he was the father. He then instructed the child how to shoot the arrows and the boy propelled each of them in a different direction. Our guide explained that this was a symbolic gesture to disperse the disease away from his body. The birds, quite satiated by then, were first disemboweled, still twitching as their guts slithered out, and finally and mercifully decapitated. The intestines were spread all over the boy's naked shoulders and back. Words were offered to the local gods in prayer and the boy was finally washed off with the remaining water in the pot. At the end of the ceremony, he walked slowly back toward the path from which he had emerged with the sheet held behind him by his mother and they disappeared from our view. I don't know what the results of the cure were but, if the kid lived through that ceremony, his chances of recovery should be quite high. This was one of the most fascinating interludes of travel I have ever had. We moved off, seemingly ignored, back to our car and on with our adventure.

Getting Adopted

There seems to be no end to the highlights I recollect in my journeys to the Third World, but some special experiences can be had almost anywhere. I include in that category the time I spent in Europe in the fifties which were as growthful, exciting and formative as my later Third World experiences. The reason was simple; I often traveled alone. That is, in itself, rife with possibilities for unforeseen adventure. Things do seem to be a bit more dangerous now for the solitary tourist but independent travel is still possible in many places. The traveler just has to be a bit more careful. I recall several times when I was traveling by myself that I met someone special who took care of me in a way that deeply enriched my experience. There many such occasions but the frequency with which such happenings occurred on a single trip in less than one month on the road offers testimony to the potential of a solitary journey. A single person is more approachable and usually perceived to be needier than individuals in a group.

On that trip, the first time I was "adopted" was on a train I took from Germany to Spain during a vacation from the school where I was teaching in Giessen, a small city just north of Frankfurt. A passenger coach connected to our train as we stopped briefly at a station in Northern Italy; it included a compartment which contained a young woman, perhaps about twenty years old (I was twenty-five at the time), who was returning to her home in Spain after a performance as a ballerina in Italy together with her mother who had gone with her as chaperone. Such supervision was a fairly common custom at that time on the Iberian Peninsula though it is not widely practiced anymore in that part of the world. My luck! Never really did shake Mom off. At any rate, Lucia, the dancer, and I became acquainted and spent a good deal of time together talking and getting to know one another. I found out that she was from Barcelona, my first stop in Spain. After we got chummy, she and her mother invited me to stay at their place while I was in the city. Of course I jumped at the chance, though my fantasies about the potential inherent in that offer were never to be fully realized.

The apartment was actually a cold water flat (Spain was rather poor in the late fifties and so was this one parent family). I had a room to myself and the two women stayed together while I was there. At the flat, there was no opportunity to be alone with Lucia but I did have a whirlwind day or so with her as she volunteered to spend her time showing me the entire town. On one outing she ordered for me at a restaurant we chose for lunch and introduced me to the seagoing, squiggly things that Barcelona specializes in - squid, octopus, snails, etc.- which I might never have otherwise gotten to include in my diet. My sensitivity to her presence prevented me from leaving any food on my plate and I have enjoyed those dishes ever since. We played games with one another other at museums like two romantic kids, we walked endlessly through the city and I wound up with a wonderful two day interlude in my journey yet we both knew this was just a passing fancy. We never did see one another again but I would not have wanted to miss those days together.

The very next stop on that same trip was Madrid. On one of the days of my sojourn there I took a local bus to the museum-like city of Toledo, a common tourist destination. Although the city itself is beautiful and its role in Spanish history is quite important, it was not the place itself that was so special to me as much as the memorable circumstances of the day. I had been working in Germany for a half year by the time I went on that trip and my German had become fairly passable. As I stepped off the bus with my guide book in tow, a youngster about eleven years of age spoke to me in Spanish. He wanted to know if he could guide me around the city. He said he knew all the important places and could tell me about them. It seemed that my day would be considerably easier without a need to navigate from place to place and he asked for very little money (the year was 1957.) I guess on this occasion, it was the kid whom I adopted for the day rather than the other way around.

As I was negotiating with my new guide, I spotted a confused German tourist who had arrived on the same bus from Madrid. It was clear that he spoke no Spanish and was looking for help in finding his way around. I went up to him and invited him to join us using my best, newly acquired German. What a day! The three of us walked the streets of Toledo together. I had my guide book for reference so I only had to be led to the important places by my young friend. Whatever he explained to me in Spanish or I read in my book in English, I then translated into German. I would say that the experience was stressful for my language skills but the challenge was exhilarating and my ability to carry it off was exciting and satisfying. It surely made for one of the most interesting travel days I experienced during my years in Europe. I was absolutely sold on language study by the end of that day's journey.

Soon after my visit to Toledo the next leg of my trip took me to Portugal. I was alone in Lisbon one evening and found my way into a local restaurant for a good Portuguese seafood meal (Is there bad Portuguese seafood?). Traveling alone can sometimes be a bit uncomfortable and eating by oneself in a place where no one else speaks your language is one of those times. I was about at the midpoint of my meal when the owner of the restaurant approached me to inquire if I spoke Portuguese. I responded in Spanish (the closest I could come) and informed him that I did not. We were able to communicate a bit in broken Spanish though the languages are fairly distinct, especially in pronunciation. He managed to convey to me that, if I wished, I could remain until the restaurant closed and he would then escort me to a non-touristy setting which I might find quite enjoyable. I had no plans for the evening and rarely turned down offers when I traveled so I stayed until his other guests left. What happened next had to be another one of the loveliest and most serendipitous evenings of my travel. We went together to a nearby Fada club. Fada is the traditional folk singing style of the area. Its closest equivalent may be the flamenco music of Spain, yet it is quite different as well. We descended into what reminded me of a cellar café in other parts of Europe. There were about thirty or so other folks in the room sitting at tables and drinking wine or beer. From time to time, one or other of the guests would just rise up and begin to sing the folk poetry that they knew by heart. My host did so several times exhibiting a mellow and tuneful voice. He was apparently a devoted aficionado of the traditional music of his country. I was transfixed by the setting, the wonderful music and the good luck I had in being there. Sometimes, taking a chance really pays off for the traveler. I have learned to be a bit more wary over the ensuing years but being overly careful is a sure way to keep oneself from experiencing such special moments. Future adoptions included a couple of weeks in London when I stayed with several British soldiers I met in Germany a year earlier who managed to take turns hosting me by procuring alternate days off from their work, an invitation to a wonderful wine tasting in a cellar in the Rhine area, meeting a child in Scotland who brought me to his home after he helped me find a local attraction I was searching for - an interesting nearby park - and whose parents housed me and toured me for a couple of days, and many other such opportunities.

Vodka, Anyone?

Another of the early highlights I experienced took place in Russia during the Cold War. This event occurred on a family vacation I took in Scandinavia one summer when our kids were quite young. While we were in Helsinki, we decided to go on a bus trip to what was then Leningrad. We had never been to Russia and the proximity was very tempting. A few of the most memorable couple of hours of that trip actually took place in the rather drab hotel where our international busload of tourists was housed. The occasion was a group dinner in the dining room of our hotel which developed into a major international trading session. At that time, blue jeans as well as most other Western clothing were at a premium in Russia. They just were not available in the stores which looked a lot like places in the States after they had been cleaned out by a fire sale. At some point, toward the end of our meal that evening, a waiter asked one of us if he would be willing to trade any clothing for vodka or caviar, two items where were quite accessible there. That began the great exchange session. We spent the next hour or more stripping and drinking, and mostly getting hysterical. By the time we finished, our table of 25 or so had consumed about a half bottle of vodka each, countless plates of caviar and snacks, laughed ourselves sick and supplied a whole group of waiters with complete Western dress. They even accepted in trade a tie I had with me which Bev was so glad to have me get rid of that she would have paid them to take it. There was a young man about 18 or 19 years old with us. The waiters really coveted his jeans which he was extremely reluctant to exchange. We finally shamed him into going up to his room, changing and bringing down the jeans. They must have been worth at least three bottles of vodka themselves. It was one of the most hilarious nights I ever remember even though it is now over 40 years ago. Not much else about Russia was funny at that time.

Welcome, Mr. Prime Minister

And then there was the night we ate with the prime minister of Papua New Guinea, or at least we dined at the next table. We returned from a trip to the Sepik Jungle area of the country on a motorboat which took us to a lodge located on the Kalawari River, a tributary of the Sepik, located in the deeply forested area. The lodge was named after the Karawari and was designed in the local style with spirit figures carved into all the bar furniture and ubiquitous, magnificent masks decorating the wall and corners of the dining room. Along the walk up a steep hill from the riverside to the lodge we passed a group of four men with what seemed to be store-bought guitars and home-made percussion instruments consisting of various lengths of bamboo cut to emit a variety of tones on the scale of music that was being played. They beat the open ends of bamboo with flip-flops which struck me as a novel idea. I had no idea at the time what they were playing or practicing but I was soon to discover the answer to that puzzle. When we reached the nearby entrance of the lodge, there was a sign that welcomed the prime minister of the country to the area and to the very lodge where he and we were to stay that night.

Later on, we found out that the PM, Julius Chan, was to address the local population early that evening on behalf of a member of his party who was running for reelection to parliament. We heard the beating of the rotors of a helicopter a few hours later and rushed down the hillside to see the arriving celebrities. Two men appeared at the edge of the crowd which filled the hill that descended toward an improvised stage further down where Chan was to address the assemblage. Chan and the Member of Parliament were being carried by a group of men on palanquins like African kings or Roman emperors. The hill was already packed with natives of the area, dressed (or more accurately "undressed") in the local custom with painted bodies, feathered headdresses and coverage of only the genital areas in the case of adults. The pre-pubescent kids were naked for the most part. We joined the crowd to listen to Chan's message which was delivered in Pidgin English[8] and probably not very widely understood by the highly decorated listeners who had traipsed many miles that day (or even more than just a single day) from hill and river villages a long distance away. Their presence was a tribute to the head of the Papua government.

When I asked my guide why I was hearing "Israel" mentioned a number of times in the speech that Chan was giving, he explained that the PM had recently been on a trip to Israel and that he saw how the people made the desert bloom. He was encouraging the gathering to work hard for their country and to make the jungle as productive as possible. Very Kennedyesque, I thought. As interesting as it was to look out over this *National*

8   Pidgin English is a form of language created to communicate between different language speaking cultures which usually are engaging in some mutual commercial undertaking. The language uses a rather simplified grammatical form. In some areas of Papua New Guinea, for example, there is a variety introduced by Australian overseers who used PNG laborers on the island to work the fields and farms in Australia. The language is widely spoken in Port Moresby, the capital of the country.

Geographic scene, it was not even the most exciting part of the day.

After the speeches and ceremony were over, we returned to our room in the lodge to prepare for dinner and the real treat of the evening. A couple of hours later the sights that greeted us in the dining room were harbingers of what was to be a truly surreal evening. The lodge was rather modest in size and the room itself housed only three or four large tables. Ours was in the center of the dining area. The big table next to ours on one side accommodated a dozen or so Japanese birders and their guide. To our left was the band we had seen earlier on the hill now dressed in local outfits from the jungle as they played the PNG music they had been practicing outside. They were all men and featured oversized penis gourds[9] as a component of their respective outfits as well as very carefully painted symbols on their bodies and faces. We constituted a group of six Americans who had met on the Sepik village segment of our journey and we sat at our own table once more that night. Soon after we were seated and served, the guest of honor arrived with his entourage which consisted of the MP we had seen earlier and three other men we did not recognize. They sat at the table on our other side. The unfamiliar music had already begun to fill the hall; the Japanese guide was calling out the names of birds that had been spotted that day while his clients were yelling out "hai" when a particular bird was recognized and then quickly checking it off in their

---

9   A penis gourd, also referred to as a "phallocrypt," is a conical object worn by some of the men of Papua New Guinea over their penis and held on by a cloth band which ties around the waist. It is constructed out of an ornamental gourd and decorated. It is used to protect the penis on an otherwise naked body and can also be used to store small things that need to be carried. It is kind of a jock strap and purse combined.

respective bird-books; a native who worked at the lodge came in to dance for us covered with a full body dance-mask, and Julius Chan and his entourage negotiated the menu. Spirit figures which decorated the room stared at us from every angle. I could not imagine a more amazing setting. We Americans joined the dancing enthusiastically and even persuaded some of the Japanese tourists to join us. This variety of undertakings and the chaos which surrounded us made for an incredible and memorable evening. Ah, serendipity.

Lest you think one must share the evening with the prime minister for a special experience in Papua New Guinea, I assure you that such is not the case at all. First of all, there are two important Highland festivals during the year to choose from for a view of the incredible variety and dress of the island and, furthermore, there are amazing customs to experience among the diverse cultures that exist all over the island. I was particularly taken with the local Wigmaster who lives in a forest and is attended to by young Huli[10] men from the hill country who wish to cultivate their hair in order to make a very valuable wig for themselves, an artifact that the culture highly values for status and special events. The job of the Wig master is to instruct these students how to grow their hair, how to cut it, and then how to weave a wig from it. When Huli warriors are not shooting arrows at one another, they spend a lot of time primping for dances and festivities of various kinds.

---

10   The Huli are an indigenous people that live in the Southern Highlands of Papua New Guinea._There are over 65,000 of the tribe and they have been living in the area for at least 600 years. The Huli family includes half-brothers, half-sisters, and cousins and they are all considered brothers and sisters. They hunt, gather plants and grow crops like sweet potatoes, corn, potatoes, and cabbage. Men and women still live separately in this culture. Men decorate their faces with colored clay and wear headdresses for ceremonies.

That activity includes both a great deal of face painting and the wearing of wigs made from human hair that they have produced or rented for a given occasion. Their wig is often decorated with priceless bird feathers, especially those of the Birds of Paradise that inhabit the hills, a custom that threatens the continued existence of these lovely creatures.

The wig master contracts with young men who come to him to exchange their labor on his behalf for a full year of hair growing instructions. The Hulis who stay with him sleep on a hard surface fashioned from logs and they lay their head on a crosswise elevated and apparently extremely uncomfortable crosspiece of wood to air their hair properly. A single wig requires a full year of residence in the forest alongside their mentor. Some of the students stay a second year to create what is essentially a double wig, an item which is twice as valuable. The rental price of these artifacts is a good source of income for the graduates of the wig school although I would personally not be inclined to invest two years in that forest for the rental business or prestige that ensues.

Great Expectations

I have ultimately come to expect wonderful experiences during my travels and, for the most part, my expectations have been fulfilled. I guess virtually all of my journeys include highlights so I could go on and on reminiscing about these adventures. I remember just riding along a road connecting the cities of Dali and Lijiang in China's southern province of Yunnan and discovering the most remarkably colorful market I have ever seen. My interest in photography has made me a lover of markets because there is so much to see and learn in them and because the scenery is so authentic and intrinsic to the life of the people who frequent them. The people at this one were

Bai tribals[11] who were all dressed in colorful, traditional clothing, the bright green rice fields that surrounded the market extended to the foothills of majestic mountains, and piles of food and materials offered for sale were quite different from what we were accustomed to seeing. As we were driving north on the road past the market, our vehicle became mired in a sudden traffic jam caused by the multitude of carts and trucks going to the market so we just indicated to our non-English speaking driver that we would see him on the other side of the market town and we just got out. We could see the worry in his expression because he was responsible for us but it all worked out well. We actually did find our car again which had only gone a mile or so after about an hour in the heavy traffic and we got to see the foods, artifacts, and various building materials in the incredible market in the interim. We were definitely the object of enormous curiosity (not unusual in China anyway, but especially the case in this rural, tribal area of the country). The only one who suffered during that incident was our driver who must have thought he would never find us again and who likely worried that his driving career was in grave jeopardy.

On still another occasion, I have a vivid memory of an opportunity we took to go into a working mine in Bolivia. It was in the old Colonial town of Potosi, once a major center

---

11   There are roughly two million Bai people, almost four fifths of whom live in communities in the Dali Bai Autonomous Prefecture in Yunnan Province, southwest China. They often dress in traditional, highly decorated, colorful outfits and they speak a language that is related to the Yi branch of the Chinese-Tibetan language family. They are one segment of the large minority population of China. The Bai people have shown outstanding skill in architecture over the centuries. The best illustration of this is the group of three pagodas at the Chongsheng Temple in Dali. These were built during the Tang Dynasty. The highest, the 16-storey main tower, is 60 meters high and over 1000 years old.

for Spanish gold mining. After we stopped at the Miner's Market to purchase a gift for the workers we anticipated encountering inside the mine, we were required to dress from head to toe in mining clothes and boots. The helmets we wore were the same as those the miners there used. Our only illumination would come from the lights attached to the helmets. We descended into the depths of a hill called *Cerro Rico,* where we experienced the conditions under which these hard-working people labor, sometimes for 24 or so straight hours. In the heart of the dark entry tunnel we stopped to pay homage at a shrine for miners who had died there and then proceeded to visit a mysterious figure made out of wood and paper mache named *Tio Pepe* who needed placating to ensure safety and success in the pursuit of gold. We learned that miners entering the site gave this icon of superstition a cigarette or a sip of local liquor or some such gift each time they entered. It was another world down there, a world of hardship and fear, hope and worship, a world we were totally unfamiliar with before our trip. But most of all it was a place where the workers remained for their long work day chewing on the local stimulant of coca leaves to keep going as they inserted small sticks of dynamite into cracks in the rock and blasted openings hoping for a sighting of the precious metal still left in the caves. It had been suggested that either dynamite sticks or bags of coca leaves would be the most appropriate gifts we could bring the workers. We choose the coca.

Another exciting time occurred in another part of the high Andean terrain. One time in our travels, we decided to park our car at a train station in Southern Ecuador to take what turned out to be a very special train ride to the colonial city of Cuenca well south of Quito down near the Peruvian border. That turned out to be a lucky choice because, in addition to a visit to a lovely old Spanish town, we got to ride on the top of a one car train curving though some of the most picturesque segments of the Andes. There was a low railing at the back of the roof where we could hold on, a ladder enabling us to ascend relatively safely, and a group of several other tourists and residents who preferred the open space and the views afforded to those of us who sat high above it all. The many turns, dizzying altitude and exceptional view all made for several of the best hours we have spent in our travels. We stopped at small towns with tiny stations and watched from above as solitary farmers and their families walked about or stood in doorways to watch the daily event of our little train passing through. We were even able to get out and spend a half hour or so in a town which was reminiscent of our Wild West, folks strolling in from the fields with their harvest at the end of the day or riding along on small horses or mules with broad brimmed hats shielding them from the sun. Their skin was hard and dark and their dress was traditional for that area and designed to protect them from the strong sun that bathes them almost every day of the year. The ride back to where we had left our car a couple of days later was no less beautiful and exhilarating.

One can also have interesting experiences without moving about at all however. One day we were in the houseboat we stayed on in Srinigar, Kashmir when there was a knock on our door. A handsome, elderly man with a full beard appeared on our porch and indicated that he was a tailor and would be happy to fashion something for us. I had not bought any good clothes for a long period of time so I listened to his offer to make me a suit. He brought several cloths from which he could fashion a woolen suit for me, he said, and he could do it quickly and cheaply. I decided to take him up on what seemed like a generous offer at a very affordable price. A couple of days later, he showed up at our houseboat once more suit in hand. I was taking a mid-day nap at the time but that was no problem for the tailor. He just sat down on the porch and waited an hour or so until I got up and became aware he was there. I could never imagine such service in the States. The suit looked nice, fit well and cost little. I gained quite a few pounds that winter and could never again locate the body that was fitted for that suit but the experience alone was probably worth the price I paid.

Shiva's Wife

As I indicated earlier, when folks ask me to encapsulate my travels through India, my response is often "India is wonder a day," an observation I make with little hyperbole. It seems to me that on any given morning one can look forward to a scene or an event or a visit that is truly startling or awe inspiring in its nature. I have described a few of my Indian escapades in this book but one that stands out in my mind is available to anyone who wishes to travel in the colorful and diverse southern part of this mysterious nation. I traveled across the South from the Indian Ocean toward the Arabian Sea and headed to the great temple in the city of Madurai named after Shiva's consort, Meenakshi. I looked forward to seeing what was reputed to be perhaps the finest of all the southern temples. It was a required stop along the way. We did not know how gratifying our experience would be.

The temples in the South are quite distinct from those in the rest of the country. They evolved from simple cave shrines carved from granite 2000 or more years ago. Over the intervening time, builders added entranceways and walls or barriers of varied structures to enclose the shrines and towers that loom high above the main structures and then they even supplemented these innovations with halls containing hundreds of sculptures and pillars. The best place to view and understand this millennia old temple development is to visit Mahabalipuram[12] not far from Chennai (formerly Madras). They are also among the great sights to behold throughout the South. But Meenakshi Temple in Madurai is arguably the finest of all. It is estimated that there are more than two million carvings scattered amongst the buildings at the site, most of which sit on the four great towers or Gopurams inside the temple area. Each individual figure is painted and meant to represent some Hindu personage or event in the ancient religious tradition. It is almost overwhelming to behold the complexity of this temple and to imagine the dedication and work that brought it into being and still keeps it ever fresh and meaningful for the worshippers. Well, that alone should be quite enough reason to go to Madurai and roam about the Meenakshi Temple. The site is also known as the Sundareshwarar which is one of the incarnations of Shiva, the ubiquitous and widely revered Hindu god who shares the temple with his consort. Visiting the site, viewing the statuary and pillars, and exploring the marvelous architecture is what tourists generally do on a visit to the city. But there is more. We spent a full morning admiring the sculpture, gazing upon 1500 year old bronze creations of heroes and gods, and walking through what is called the Thousand Pillar Hall with its plethora of carved equestrian columns. We saw the amazing statues of Shiva and Meenakshi and we observed the clever way one can make offerings to these revered figures. Since they are high, they are out of reach of visitors, so there is a vendor in front of the statues who sells small balls of butter which float in a bucket before him. These can be purchased for a pittance and then hurled at

12   Mahabalipuram is a town of ancient shore temples located on the Bay of Bengal about 40 miles from Chennai (formerly Madras) in South India. There are several famous temples at Mahabalipuram including the Shore Temple and the 'Ratha' Cave Temples which are the best known.

the figures in a gesture of offering. They stick onto the large statues so that, by the end of each day, both gods are covered with butter and, I assume, quite satiated with their offerings. Then comes cleanup time after which the same ritual repeats itself the next day. That alone was a remarkable sight and we were delighted to witness this longstanding tradition and watch the devotees to whom it was so important. But even that was not all the temple had to offer.

Believe it or not, there was still one more remarkable observation to be made at Meenakshi, surely the most amazing of all. We returned to the temple later that day. There was a brief downpour the afternoon we visited the temple and we had to take off our shoes and socks to slosh through the puddles that had formed on the walkway into the temple while we were resting in our room that afternoon. We did not mind that mild inconvenience because we were returning to the site in the evening to see an event which takes place every one of the 365 evenings of the year. After the tourists have left and darkness begins to blanket Madurai, a group of Brahmins, the caste of men who perform the required Hindu rituals, assemble at Shiva's shrine along with several musicians, a few devotees and a handful of other visitors who come to see the ceremony. The Brahmins enter Shiva's holy space (Hindus believe that the living spirit of a god resides within his or her shrine) and lift the symbol of Shiva, the *lingam*, a phallic object which represents his presence, to gently place it into a decorated palanquin which they then put on their shoulders. From there the unique parade winds its way through the now darkened temple all the way to the other side of the building where Meenakshi's shrine is located. The *lingam* is then removed from its colorful enclosure mounted on the palanquin to the accompaniment of music and chanting and kneeling worshippers lining the path and is finally brought to Meenakshi so that the two gods may bed together for the night.

Apparently, living spirits also have living emotions including carnal ones. In the morning, the Brahmin's return once again to place Shiva in his daytime location by reversing the process. Relatively few travelers to Madurai get to see this unbelievable ritual. We will never forget it.

Even a Detour Can Be a Highlight

Events like those we witnessed at the Meenakshi Temple are not guaranteed to pop up for visitors just because they have journeyed to the farthest corners of the earth. Our personal world has kept expanding with each new encounter, with every story we learned, with every bit of knowledge we gathered. The Third World is indeed a place full of mystery and wonder. We have discovered that even unsuccessful endeavors can produce surprisingly interesting consequences. A good example of this was a trip to the Philippines we took one summer. Our plan was to spend a month beginning in the Manila area at festival time, then head out to visit the Ifugao people who live in the northern section of Luzon and to view their wonderful terraced rice fields and traditional culture, then go south to several islands with beautiful coasts and other tribal societies. Little of that plan ever materialized. We did get to Manila and we did visit several interesting harvest festivals in small towns near the capitol, every one of which we endured in a constant rain. The downpours never stopped. We have been extremely lucky with the weather on our travels for the most part so we did not feel at all sorry for ourselves; we just got very wet. We watched in the rain, we danced in the rain, we walked in the rain and we shopped in the rain. After a few days, we became aware of several facts. First of all, the monsoons had arrived at least a month early. We were informed that we could not depend on the rain stopping any day soon. Nonetheless, at the end of the week, we tried to head north. No luck there either. We approached the first toll gate on the highway leading toward the northern area of the Island of Luzon and were turned away. There were floods throughout the North, we were told, and no one was permitted to go onto the highway. Meanwhile, we had been reading regularly in the local newspapers about the terrorist activity in the South where government forces were fighting rebel Muslims who wanted to separate the southern islands from the rest of the country. We found out that even the airport we were supposed to fly into had been bombed by rebels and was dangerously pockmarked. Tourists had been kidnapped and apparently killed in some cases. Although we were not in the immediate neighborhood at the time, there was even a terrorist bombing at a shopping center we had visited earlier in the day in Manila.

I am far from a nervous traveler but that was enough for me. I was not dismayed when Bev said, "Get me out of here!" A trip to the office of the tourist agency where we had booked some reservations settled things. They were very understanding and refunded the remainder of what we had paid for our trip. We decided to just get a flight and use the next three weeks somewhere else. There was a convenient departure to Spain which we secured and boarded the very next day. Although I had been to Spain twice many years earlier, Bev had never visited the country. We had not yet begun the free cruise ship sailings I describe in another chapter which enabled us to return to Europe after a very long hiatus. We landed in Madrid, rented a car, and then meandered through the Iberian Peninsula for three weeks and had a wonderful time. It was not the Third World but it was not as expensive as most of Europe was during a later summer we returned to the area. Bev loved it and I too enjoyed revisiting the site of some earlier travels and getting a little more practice in Spanish. It was also interesting to see the changes in the countryside since I had last been there. When we told our son over the phone that we were going to Europe, he said, "You will never get Mommy back to the Third World after this." His comment was meant to be facetious but travel is much easier and more dependable in the West. Nonetheless, things turned out just fine. We continued to explore the less visited parts of the world for the following years of our travel and enjoyed those trips as much or more than Iberia. That is no reflection on Spain or Portugal (part of the trip took us there also) which are interesting and colorful and far more familiar than lands to the south or east.

Weddings and funerals and other Surprises

If you do the unexpected, like driving along roads where there have been virtually no tourists, you will surely uncover the unexpected. I hark back to the day I was in the heart of Sumatra, Indonesia and had several hours of free time. Surely, one's hotel room at Lake Toba, in the heart of the tribal area of one of the groups of the patrilineal Batak[13] people is no place to while away an afternoon. Instead, we asked our driver to take us for an afternoon's ride on the road that circled the island although most of the road was well off the usual trail. About half way around, we encountered a bridge which was primarily just two rails, each one not much thicker than the tires of our van and some broken wooden cross boards and rickety fencing to either side. Now I knew why the road was not better traveled. Nonetheless, we got out and walked over the bridge while our driver was guided along the rails following us. Soon after that mini-adventure, we passed a group of people going

13   The Batak people live in the northern section of the island of Sumatra in Indonesia. Although their culture is relatively traditional, they are also considered to be the largest protestant community in Asia. There are over 4,000,000 of them and they are known for their good guitar playing and singing. They constitute six groups with rather distinct differences in customs among them.

up a hill heading toward some apparently well attended event. I asked the driver to inquire about what was happening and he reported back to me that there was a funeral at the top and that the sponsors cordially invited us to join them at the ceremony. That is just the sort of encounter that I have come to value most. We climbed out of our car and were escorted to the site by several people who were also on their way up the hill. We had evidently not only stumbled onto something special but were there at just the right time. As we climbed, we passed several tented areas where soda and food were being disbursed and we were very sincerely welcomed to partake of the offerings.

At the top of the hill there were hundreds of people assembled. On the far edge of the site was an elevated miniature house which looked just like the actual ones the people on the island lived in. We understood that it was to be the final burial site for the deceased. The host welcomed us and invited us to participate in the dancing that was going on. We did so mimicking the steps and the activities of the other attendees. Meanwhile, a group of bare-chested young boys and men provided the music from a small balcony on a building just behind the dancing area. People seemed to enjoy our presence about as much as we enjoyed being in such a different and fascinating setting. They insisted we eat before leaving which we did. When we finally had to go, we were accompanied by 30 or so children who descended the hill with us and waved goodbye as we departed in our car. Just another experience in the Third World. Another couple of miles along the road we again saw a funeral in progress. This second discovery was an example of an initial burial that takes place just after the person dies, and it consisted of a smaller group of people in what we would more easily recognize as mourning. They sat about in prayer and mutual consolation and their food and manner were considerably more low key than where we had just come from. Imagine - a short ride around the island - one incredible bridge, one full scale burial celebration/village party and one active funeral. That helped us while away the afternoon all right.

I have no idea what the reader is likely to consider as highlights should he or she follow in our tracks but the world does grow culturally smaller every day. The accessible traditional societies, whether they be in tortured wildernesses in Africa, remote villages in the Andes, the islands of Indonesia or tribal areas of India or New Guinea or Burma or the Amazon are more and more impacted by the surrounding culture and the advent of advanced technology and communication. Basically, if one does not get there soon, it may not be worth going. The Third World is not waiting for us to discover its riches; it is steadily changing every day. Curious travelers have to pack up their store of sensitivity, energy, curiosity and respect for others and get moving along.

CHAPTER FOUR

SURVIVAL

"The traveler was active; he went strenuously in search of people, of adventure, of experience. The tourist is passive; he expects interesting things to happen to him. He goes 'sight-seeing.' "
— **Daniel J. Boorstin**

The opposite of experiencing highlights is living through and even occasionally finding something worthwhile on a trip in the face of peril and potential calamity. It is not always easy or comfortable traveling in the Third World. One might even say that uncertainty and challenge are elements of the typical experience one has traipsing through the less developed parts of our globe. My mind flashes back to many moments when we had to muck our way through a measure of unpleasantness and even a few times when we were not sure we would make it.

The Houseboat
The Mahakam River winds slowly down to the sea from the mountains of Central Borneo (the province of Kalimantan in Indonesia) to the Makassar Strait where it deposits its accumulated soil and nutriments into the Delta near the city of Balikpapan. Since the river is navigable all the way

into the jungle, it is available for transporting goods and carrying occasional tourist expeditions for whom a couple of houseboat-like vessels ply its waters. This is a quite out of the way tourist route however. Jungle sites and scenes, traditional village life, and a sense of solitude and adventure were all enticements for this trip so we decided to undertake it during a visit to the island.

Our meander up the Mahakam was one of several times that Bev said to me, "You are never going to do this to me again!" I really could not blame her for that remark. The adventure started out as a simple, laid-back activity - a houseboat, a river, villages to visit, sights to be photographed and so on. We were unaware that there would be anything to be concerned about.

We arrived from Balikpapan at the river docks a couple of miles away about two o'clock in the afternoon. We boarded an older craft (actually I do not remember seeing any new ones) and were soon on our way. The crew of three (captain, cook, and guide) would assure a safe and informative voyage, or so we thought. We were not much more than an hour or so underway when we heard a heavy clunk underneath our boat. I was told that one of the many logs we saw floating down the river had damaged the propeller and we needed to stop at the next port to replace it. I guess I should have taken that as an omen and said "Take us back" but it never occurred to me to do so. Our ship limped into a small village port about an hour further up the river. The captain got out to speak with a few people at the dock and determined that there was no available replacement for our propeller but that there was another even simpler, more basic houseboat that we could switch to and that was what we decided to do. We finally got underway on the second vessel in the late afternoon.

The rest of the evening went along just fine. The first full day included visits to dramatically unusual villages where as many as a hundred tribal people lived together in common longhouses in extended families or clans. Their society was marked by sparse traditional dress and by customs that very recently included headhunting (the rumor was that it still existed) among other singular cultural practices. The things we saw and what we learned that day seemed well worth the minor aggravation of the previous afternoon. As we set sail up the river the second night toward the deeper jungle and more remote villages, the breeze took the edge off the otherwise oppressive humidity and provided us comfort in the open boat, that is until darkness arrived, the sky clouded over and logs in the river seemed to multiply exponentially. When a heavy rain began to descend from the blackened sky, the ship slowed to almost a full stop because the captain could not see more than a few feet in front of us.

Until that time, we were relatively unaware of the excessive heat outside and quite unaffected by the multitude of insects that winged by us carried swiftly on the passing breeze. When we slowed down and closed the canvas that protected us from the rainfall, the world around us changed considerably. It must have been about 95 degrees or more outside and we were surrounded and attacked by thousands of little flying things. The heat and humidity became overwhelming and we began to have bites on bites from the host of crawly, creepy guests we were accumulating. This was, perhaps, our most unpleasant evening of travel although a few others do compete for first place. At any rate, there would be no sleep for us that night. But at least we did not have another broken propeller experience along the way. We somehow avoided the large shards of vanishing forest that floated in the current toward us. As we looked out into the darkness from time to time, we were able to appreciate what it must have been like for the residents of the tiny dimly lit villages we passed along the sides of the river to live in such a challenging environment.

The rainforest itself which lay just behind the shore must have been insufferable for those who lived there their entire lives.

All was not lost on the Mahakam. Our visits were very informative and interesting; we survived the bugs and heat and we knew it could not get much worse than it was during that night on our houseboat. The memories of that adventure were well fixed in our minds yet we were to invite such potential discomfort on many subsequent occasions. But the knowledge we gained about the nature of headhunting and the visits we made to longhouses where groups of so many extended families or clans sheltered together for communal protection actually even made the horrible night worthwhile.

Robbers

Although one can get robbed anywhere in the world (I found an extra hand in one of my pockets in Barcelona and another in Brazil for example), in poor countries, the traveler is a walking invitation for desperate people to enhance the quality of their lives by taking great risks. Expensive cameras dangle from tourist shoulders, fanny packs stir curiosity and invite investigation, bulging pockets tempt the shrewd and needy, and the idea that one needs to be rich to come so far sets up a far greater likelihood of reward for robbery of visitors in the backwaters of the world. We have had several experiences with intrepid thieves along our travel paths. Pickpocketing is the most basic mode of theft and we have been quite lucky in this regard. We got away without loss in Barcelona and in Rio as well. I grabbed at the respective hands just in time. One unusual experience does stand out in this respect however. Along a rather deserted street about three blocks from our hotel in a small colonial city in Bolivia, we were walking along toward a restaurant after dark when I felt some liquid land on my head. I did not see anyone else on the street so I looked up at the small balcony on the house right next to the one where I stood when I noticed the wet feeling but the balcony was quite empty. As I took out something to wipe my head I noticed a man not more than a few feet away whom I did not see before. Just about the same time, two Indian Bolivianas with their traditional hoop skirts and colorful local dress came walking toward us on the very narrow sidewalk of the street and brushed by me. I was alerted by the unlikelihood that they would choose to physically make contact with me since they were more prone to be deferential to foreigners than to crowd them. I felt movement as one of them touched the fanny pack I was wearing which contained my passports. I was not carrying any money in the pack but the passports were enough to worry about. I immediately checked by feeling the pack and noted that the passports were already gone. The whole event had taken a matter of seconds to that point. As soon as I realized what had happened (a clever and bold setup), I grabbed the woman in front of me and shouted at her that she had better return the passports or we were headed to the police- a good time to use my Spanish skills. She pleaded innocence but since I was not letting go, she finally disclosed that my passports were on the hood of the car parked right next to us. She had managed in an instant to transfer them to her partner who saw her distress and placed them there. The man had already disappeared. We never did go to the police. Our itinerary required us to leave the town early the next morning and we did not want to get involved in a long term process. The woman was quite frightened and I was upset enough to want the whole thing to end. This all transpired so quickly that Bev, who was only a few steps away from me, had no idea of what happened until I explained it all as we walked the additional half block toward the restaurant. It was an assault well worthy of cocktail conversation but not one I would encourage anyone to invite. Walking around in the dark on relatively isolated streets is generally not a good idea anywhere in the world.

Bandito Attack

By far the most dramatic and dangerous robbery I ever experienced was an improbable encounter with bandits as we returned to Belize from the spectacular Mayan site of Tikal in Guatemala. It was a rainy afternoon and we were on our way back after a muddy Tikal visit. The road we were on was slippery and empty. In our travel van were Bev and I and two friends, as well as a few other tourists - about nine of us in all. Roughly half way back to the border, the van pulled to a stop in front of a kerchiefed bandit pointing an AK-47 at us and motioning for us to pull up. The driver seemed quite stunned and nervously instructed us to give the robbers whatever they wanted and not say anything to them. While the man who stopped us kept his gun pointed at the driver from outside, within a few seconds the door opened and two other bandits with guns and machetes leaped into the van and went from person to person demanding anything of value that we had with us. Fortunately, only one person had anything to be concerned about so our collective wisdom about not carrying valuables on Third World travel had served us well. The woman who suffered the misfortune of carrying valued items lost a ring and a bracelet that had sentimental meaning for her as she reinforced our belief that the Third World is hardly a place to roam about with family heirlooms.

When the robbers pointed a gun at my head and demanded money, it was clear from their actions that they were in more of a hurry than we were. I reached into my pocket, took out a few loose bills in the local currency and handed it to him. He did not stop to count. They did take my wife's point and shoot camera but I told them my SLR was not working and, amazingly, they left it. It was big and possibly too complicated or bulky for them anyway so they did not seem to mind my suggestion that it was a worthless object to carry. As a matter of fact, it was the only thing I had that I did value. My friend who had fallen asleep before the incident began, awoke during the commotion and opened his eyes to find a machete at his neck and a robber pointing to his pocket. Quite a rude awakening as they say. The whole interaction lasted but a few minutes and the robbers quickly fled back into the forest thicket. We came to understand later that they would have been shot on sight had the police come by during the robbery so I assume their haste was quite justified. Later on, after we all started breathing again, we did stop at a Guatemalan police station along the way to report the robbery. Somehow, I was not sure there was no connection between those who wrote down the information at that outpost and those who robbed us and disappeared into the jungle but I had an eerie feeling that complicity could have been another aspect of the total operation. When we returned to Belize, we heard that such robberies were not uncommon. Funny, they did not tell us that when we signed up for the trip.

My Shoes, my Shoes

The most humorous, albeit annoying, robbery that happened to me occurred at a Buddhist festival in Kataragama, a town in southern Sri Lanka. We attended a pilgrimage festival or *Perihera* as it is called locally which featured colorful parades, decorated elephants and thousands of devout worshippers and took place in a small market town. The event was attended by Hindus and Buddhists alike although a civil war was raging between the two communities. It was a delightful experience for us until we returned from the enclosure where the main events took place. One had to leave shoes at the entranceway as is customary at the holy places of both religious groups. Our guide instructed us to do so before we entered the temple grounds. I asked him about the safety of our shoes which stood out among the countless sets of old flip-flops made mostly of recycled rubber tire pieces. I was concerned because we intended to spend several hours inside. He assured me unequivocally that there was no danger anyone would steal shoes at such an event. That risk cost me a good, but somewhat dirty, pair of Rockport walking shoes, the only serviceable footwear I had brought with me on the trip. They were no longer there when we left. Back to our hotel in socks. Oh, well, so much for knowledgeable guides and respect for holy sites. It was not so much the loss of the shoes that bothered me, but we had a couple of days left on our trip which I had to endure shoelessly. My sandals had to do for the rest of the time aggravating my flat feet considerably. It was a great festival however and the elephants were magnificent. Glad we did not miss it. If the reader finds some farmer in Sri Lanka walking about in a pair of Rockports, please let me know.

Our very strangest robbery of all occurred in 1968 in Budapest. We drove up to the entrance of the stately, prewar hotel we had booked for our stay in the city. We took all the things out of the car that we had brought for our summer long trip through Europe including a few practical items that are not usually part of the traveler's equipment in order to accommodate the two young children we had with us. One such item was a small hotplate which was for those occasions when we could not find appropriate food for our youngest child. We put our belongings down on the sidewalk in front of the hotel under Bev's supervision while I went in to check our reservations. It was a matter of just a few minutes before a porter came out to take our luggage inside. We soon discovered that our hotplate was missing. Those were hard times in Hungary but we never expected the hotplate to be such a highly desired object. It was one thing we never replaced on that voyage yet we all survived the loss.

Baggage Handlers

You can lose baggage anywhere in the world from Kennedy Airport to Buenos Aires to the Mediterranean. The difference is that near Kennedy there are all kinds of clothing stores from Banana Republic to K-Mart (our more likely choice) and you can replace your belongings in mid-travel without difficulty. If you are heading home, you have time to take care of your losses without difficulty so the inconvenience is minimal. However, in the midst of a planned trip with flights and hotels reserved, losing suitcases is another matter altogether. Amazingly, we only had this experience during a trip two times in a lifetime of journeys.

The first such event was on our trip to Papua New Guinea. One of our suitcases got misplaced in the airport in Sydney, Australia and we did not get it back until our return flight passed through the city again. As it turned out, except for a few items, there was little in the suitcase that we absolutely needed since the people in most of the villages we visited were half-naked anyway. We borrowed a few items from fellow travelers and did just fine. Our second experience was a bit more dramatic. Flights from Cairo to Nairobi on Ethiopian Airways include some element of risk in several respects. In our case, the most significant happening was that our entire luggage was missing upon arrival in Nairobi. We were scheduled to leave the airport from there and head straight off to Tanzania for a safari scheduled for the very next day. Needless to say, we could not do that without at least one change of clothes. Bev and I were given about fifty dollars at the airport from Ethiopian Airlines to shop for the safari and out we went. We successfully found a local place with truly basic prices (it felt like an old Five and Ten

Cent store) where we bought a couple of pairs of underwear, several t-shirts, two or three pairs of cheap socks and an extra pair of shorts. The material was quite flimsy but the items did seem sufficient to tide us over for the few days after which we expected to be receiving our luggage. With our new found wardrobe, we were able to outfit ourselves with enough clothes to change each day and wash each night. We almost always wash our daily wear each evening anyway.

We also had some luck. This was one of the few times we were with fellow travelers because we were going on a group safari. After we shared our dilemma with the other dozen or so people we were with at the lodge in Tanzania, the group's generosity was universal. With a shirt or two from a few fellow travelers and a couple of extra pairs of socks, we managed to survive the Serengeti and keep relatively clean for the next ten days. The Maasai we encountered along the way unquestionably possessed fewer changes of clothing for their daily routine than we now had packed in our luggage. When we returned to Nairobi for the rest of our trip, our suitcases were waiting and the catastrophe was weathered. That experience taught us to pack even more lightly thereafter.

The Flight from Hell

Flying to the safari via Nairobi where our baggage failed to show up was an experience in itself. First of all, we left for the trip from Tel Aviv, Israel on an El Al plane whose passengers were discharged in an out of the way area of the airport in Cairo under extremely heavy security. Apparently, El Al is not the most popular airline flying into the city. From the plane, we were taken to a transit area to enable us to continue on our way. The transit section was one of the most run down and distasteful places we had ever experienced. It was filthy, the toilets were barely tolerable, the temperature inside was overwhelmingly hot and we had virtually no communication with the other passengers waiting there, most of them on their way to the Hajj. Thank goodness for Bushra.

Bushra was a young man about 15 years of age who spoke English fluently. He was a native of the Sudan and he explained that he was transiting from Poland where his father served in the Sudanese diplomatic service. He was alone on his way back to Khartoum from Warsaw. We became friendly and Bushra was enormously helpful, translating, helping me find information about our flight and even ushering me through a small, interesting Egyptian museum contained in the transit building that he was familiar with from a prior flight. The experience would have been far more agonizing without him, especially since Air Ethiopia provided no useful information about our increasingly late flight. Thanks to Bushra, we were at least able to understand each of the announcements even though few of them conveyed the truth. Apparently, our flight was right outside ready to leave except...there was a strike in the Khartoum airport according to Air Ethiopia and we could not take off until that was resolved because we were scheduled to stop there. They kept changing their mind about whether or not to go without stopping in Khartoum and fly straight to Nairobi where we were heading, or to wait a while longer and keep their regular schedule. Poor Bushra was unable to find out if he was even getting home that afternoon. We got on the plane, only to get back off after about an hour of waiting on the tarmac seated in what seemed like 100 degree heat with no air conditioning. When our sweat soaked bodies returned to the transit area, we weren't sure where we would spend that night. The thought of doing so in the waiting room we came back to was repulsive.

Another announcement, about two hours later, indicated that the flight was going straight to Nairobi, not stopping in Khartoum, and leaving right away. Except for the Khartoum passengers, we were soon back on board. Before the airplane door finally closed, however, I was surprised to see Bushra coming down the aisle. The previous decision had been reversed again and now we were going to Khartoum. The engine finally started and the next phase of that adventure began. So what happened to the strike? I think the answer is that there was probably no strike to begin with. It was more likely that some mechanical issue was discovered, one they preferred to avoid providing any information about. The on-plane announcements left us all even more uncertain about the final decision regarding Khartoum anyway. My wife fell asleep instantly and I probably would have also had I not noted that there was a crack in the glass in my window, an observation that kept me up thinking and worrying for about an hour.

Well, we did stop in Khartoum after all but we now had to change planes which was not the original arrangement. As they transferred the luggage to our new flight destined for Nairobi, Bev nervously looked over the suitcases being carried to the plane we had transferred to from our window. She did not see ours and was frantically trying to find out if they were onboard. She was unable to do so, her observation about their absence was correct and thus we wound up going on our safari later on without any clothing. Goodbye, Bushra and the Sudan. Goodbye clothing. Our future reservations have never again included Air Ethiopia and I suspect they never will. That was clearly the proverbial flight from hell. We finally did arrive in Nairobi, many hours late, absolutely filthy and exhausted and without anything but our toilet articles as possessions.

The Gaza Gaze

We have been to Israel several times to visit family as well as to pursue our ongoing interest in the country.

Although Israel is highly developed and not at all a third world nation overall, quite a few of its citizens live under Third World conditions so the flavor and occasionally the risks one can encounter are not as remote as one might imagine. At various times in the history of the country there have been significant fluctuations in the level of tension between the Israelis and the Arabs although ill feeling is basically ever present. One can imagine the hostility that existed in the Arab Community after the war of 1967. We first visited the land just a few months after the war took place during which Israel conquered and occupied the West Bank, Gaza, the Sinai and the Golan Heights. It was our winter vacation trip during the year I taught in Rome so we had our two children with us, one of whom was 22 months old and the other almost seven years.

When we got to Tel Aviv, I rented a car and just started driving to all the many tourist sites. We began in the North and went from the Lebanese border all the way down to Eilat on the shores of the Red Sea. I guess my judgment had not matured fully by that time (it probably still has not yet done so) because I thought a look at the Gaza Strip would be quite interesting. It was indeed. We casually drove into Gaza City, got our kids out of the car and started walking along the main market street. I guess we did not fool anyone into thinking we were just friendly visitors because the stares we got were anything but welcoming. I don't often feel threatened or intimidated, but an increasing level of discomfort manifested itself. I was feeling crowded by the passersby who seemed to radiate hostility. We quickly got back to the car, packed the kids in and headed out of there. It was with a distinct sigh of relief that we motored out of Gaza that afternoon. I think I understood well the mood of the people there but I had somehow not anticipated that it would be turned toward me or my family. I hope that helped to improve my planning for the trips that followed.

Dragon Dragging

Another occasion that was probably more titillating than actually life threatening occurred on the Island of Komodo in Indonesia. We were exploring the string of islands east of Bali called Nusa Tenggara and our boat ride out of Sumbawa took us to the neighboring island famous for its "dragons," the gigantic and quite dangerous monitor lizards that populate it. This enormous, fearsome carnivore lives on only a couple of the 13,000 islands that make up the Indonesian archipelago. Our first realization that we were not in a contained or protected area arose immediately when we stepped onto the beach and saw long, thin depressions in the sand. We asked the guide what those markings were and he casually explained that they were lines made by the tails of the lizards dragging after them that morning as they crossed over the area. So we really were sharing the same space! No problem; the island hosted many groups of visitors throughout the year. We had not heard of a single untoward incident although there apparently were such tales to be told.

It was a couple of hours later when a group of us, about a dozen or so curious adventurers, gathered for the trek to see the monsters. We were accompanied by an island guide who walked next to us pulling a goat along tied to a leash. The goat bleated continuously the entire way and with very good reason. He was to be slaughtered and thrown from an overhang on a hill to an open area below to insure that we actually got to see the dragons. They would be only too happy to come out of the woods where they customarily stayed in order to tug apart and devour the gift of the goat. Four of them entered the competition. That was interesting but rather gory. They were certainly formidable looking creatures, some as big as ten or more feet long, with powerful tails, quite impressive teeth and jaws, and dripping a poisonous, bacterial saliva meant to quickly immobilize their prey.

After the goat sacrifice, our group started to stroll back toward the beach. We had a rather hazy realization that there were dragons around us although they were not in our vision but we did not have much of an idea of how shy or aggressive they might be. We did see a few signs informing us that one must beware of them yet what did that mean when the entire island hosted tourists on a regular basis? Besides, the guide was there to protect us, wasn't he? He even carried a thin, forked wooden pole to fend off attack. I asked to see it, marveled at its flimsy construction and the guide suggested that I hold it for the rest of the walk. I had no idea what to do with it should danger occur but I had also not developed any faith that it would be helpful to him either. Anyhow, it looked like a prop and was probably carried just to increase our excitement and awe at the island and its inhabitants. We were only ten minutes away from the goat-feeding scene when right before us on the opposite side of a path no more than fifteen feet away perched a fully grown lizard just staring at the approaching line of tourists. The guide directed us to keep on the far side of the path (duh!) which we were quite happy to do. I quickly gave him his protective stick back and we walked briskly by the creature. The look we received was rather intimidating and we fervently hoped this was one of the group that was satiated with fresh goat. We learned that these animals will attack humans and are quite capable of knocking someone down with their potent tail and that they can swallow large prey whole like the wild deer they feed on customarily. We breathed more easily when we left the lizard behind us still staring but we did not possess the innocence with which we began our hike that day. Had we just come from some Hollywood set or were we but a few yards from a man-eating monster? The question hung in the air, and it was not the first or last time in our travels that we faced down something quite scary. I did learn a bit later that not everyone who visited Komodo was so lucky. Recently, an article I came across on the internet read as follows:

> *Two Komodo dragons have mauled a fruit picker to death after he fell out of a tree in an orchard in eastern <u>Indonesia</u> in a rare attack on humans by the world's largest lizard.*
>
> *The man, Muhamad Anwar, 31, was found bleeding from bites to his hands, body, legs and neck within minutes of falling out of a sugar-apple tree on the island of Komodo and died later at a clinic on neighboring Flores. The giant lizards had been waiting for him under the tree, according to a neighbor, Theresia Tawa...*
>
> *Though they rarely attack humans – and had not previously killed an adult for more than 30 years – an eight-year-old boy died after being mauled in 2007 and attacks are said to be increasing as their habitat becomes restricted. Their diet usually consists of smaller <u>animals</u>, including other members of their own species.*

So much for guarding the group with the guide's forked stick.

The Flood in China

We entered China on our second trip to the country where its border meets Pakistan. That entry point brings the traveler into the westernmost province of the land along the Karakorum Highway, and that commenced our most adventurous and memorable visit. The area is called the Xinjiang Uyghur Autonomous Region, home of several minorities including the largest Muslim groups in the diverse nation. I guess the Chinese thought that calling this area "autonomous" would make the people feel free and independent. It obviously did not achieve that goal. The Chinese have not been very successful in getting most of their many minority groups to love them. This very un-touristy area was and still is antagonistic toward government rule from Beijing and there is an active resistance movement labeled "terrorist" by the central authorities, especially among the seven million or so Uygur[14] people, as is evidenced by the large number of Chinese military one sees encamped from place to place. When I inquired of my government licensed guide about the abundance of military alongside the desert, she responded that there had been some murders and they were securing the area. Murders, indeed! They were there to control the Uyghurs, not for any other reason.

Along the way we visited the wonderful market town of Kashgar in a car that must have been ten or more years old and then we headed to smaller towns in even more remote areas on one of the ancient trails of the Silk Road. I remember the leg of the ride which followed Kashgar quite distinctly because we had a flat tire midway to the next town. We were in an extremely desolate area and the guide explained to us that he did not want to get stuck there. No problem, we had a serviceable spare tire and we were only 100 or so miles from the next stop. But that turned out to be a very long 100 miles.

The car apparently had not undergone a thorough safety check before we departed on this stretch of the ride.

---

14   The Uyghurs are a Turkic speaking, ethnic group living in the northwestern region of China. They number over 7,000,000. Uyghurs are not Han Chinese but a distinctly European race and look primarily like Western Europeans. Some are in rebellion against the government of China. A number of them were incarcerated in Guantanamo Bay Prison by the Americans.

In another 25 miles or so, our driver stopped and got out to look at one of the other tires. A slow leak! We could never go the whole way without some attention to the problem. Miracle of miracles, the driver took an air compressor out of his trunk, plugged it into the cigarette lighter socket and began to pump up the leaking tire. Ah, modern technology! Could we make the remaining 75 miles before us? Would the battery last longer than the tires? The process involved our stopping about every 10-15 miles, pumping more air into the tire, getting back into the car and limping along for another prayerful segment of the journey. To our amazement and relief, we eventually drove to our hotel in the next town. The driver took the car into a mechanic for tire repair and we were back at full strength (whatever that was) for the next morning's lap. What a fine tourist infrastructure we had thrust ourselves into the middle of! But the year was 1996 - well before fancy tourist services were developed primarily motivated by the upcoming Olympics. It turned out that the tire problem was to be the easy part of that journey.

The most dangerous moment of all of our travels was before us. We should have had an inkling of what was to come when we were stopped at the end of a long line of parked cars and trucks and had to pause for quite a while. We had been rolling along and suddenly ran into a traffic jam on an otherwise relatively empty road. Although this was supposedly a highway, it was not exactly a major route for travel or transport. But we were backed up at least a quarter mile. We got out and walked along the row of disgruntled drivers sitting behind the wheels of their vehicles to discover, of all things, a rivulet some 15 or so feet wide and several feet deep. The water was coming from the snow covered Tian Shan mountains lying north of us. We assumed there was either a rainstorm or a sudden melt. The water had traveled several miles before it temporarily closed the road in front of us. And this occurred in one of driest places in the world. Finally the little river disappeared into the sandy surfaces alongside the road and traffic once again began to move. The next couple of days, we drove through a series of small market cities and ancient ruins along this ancient pathway of the old East-West Silk Road until we reached the city of Turpan.

Turpan, or *Turfan* as it is called in the local Uygur language, is a small, very old market town. It is also the second lowest depression on the Earth's surface after the Dead Sea. From here I anticipated soon arriving back to "civilization" in Xinjiang's largest city, Urumchi, where we had a room reserved in the Holiday Inn. If you don't think that is fancy, you should see the places we had been staying along the Silk Road in both Pakistan and China. Urumchi was about a three hour ride through the mountains from Turpan so we were getting close. We reached the direct road which turned out to be a very hilly and poorly constructed temporary byway. The path wound along a dry river bed that looked like it was formed a very long time ago. We had no inkling of what was to befall us.

The Waters Arrive

We were moving along relatively briskly in the junker with the two repaired tires when we were surprised to see a trickle of water beginning to flow down the center of the parched river bed. There was not a cloud in the sky so it was obviously coming from far away. The Turpan area is not only one of the lowest places in the world, it is also about as dry a locale as one can find. The city sits at the edge of the Gebi or *Taklamakan* Desert (in the local language the latter name means "He who goes in, does not come out"). But the trickle grew and grew as we wound our way north. It was soon a creek, and not long after that, a stream. We began to see the sky darken in front of us and the gush of water was quickly spreading wider in the previously empty river bed. We were impressed by how quickly the landscape was changing. It became apparent that we were driving right into a flash storm which packed quite a bit of rain.

As we gazed out of the car window, we realized that the flow was advancing rapidly and had actually reached and begun to climb the banks of the river bed in the very short time we had been observing it. We continued to move along as did the trucks and other vehicles on our road. To our marked dismay the water climbed to the edge of the flimsy looking road we were traveling on and was soon actually surging across the road in front of us. At one point we faced a crisis of significant proportion. We reached a small elevation and were confronted with a dip in the road in front of us that was already water covered. We had no idea how deep the plunge would be. The four of us needed to decide very quickly how to proceed. Just over that dip was a hill that looked to be the safest area we could reach. It was a highly desired elevated location. Since we knew we were not going to be able to continue much farther, we decided to take the risk of driving through the growing gully facing us so the driver gunned the car and into the water we went.

We stopped dead right in middle of the growing channel and the water gushed by rapidly. As we sat there, totally helpless, the water began to seep into the car and was soon above our ankles. We had been watching various objects floating down the river past us earlier and we envisioned ourselves soon following in their wake. (We later learned that a group of soldiers drowned in the river that day.) We could not move an inch. If we got out, we would likely be swallowed by the rushing stream. If we stayed, we were certainly doomed because the water was still rising rapidly. I got lucky enough to be able to make it out of there it to write this narrative. Just in front of us was a van which belonged to the same travel agency as the one we had engaged to provide our car and driver. I am not sure if any other was available. The drivers of the two vehicles knew one another and the van driver became aware of our distress. He had just made it to the edge of the hill. He quickly got out of his vehicle and motioned to our driver. Our driver held on to the car as tightly as he could and made his way rapidly to the front where a rope was tossed to him by his friend from the van. He somehow was able to tie it around the front bumper of our car, fasten it securely and return to his seat in the car in the nick of time. The van started up and pulled us slowly out of the ditch we were stuck in to higher and safer ground. We wound up several feet above the crest of the river whose grasp we had barely escaped. I guess one cannot encounter much more intensity in their travel experiences. I would never wish to face disaster so vividly again.

On the Hill

But this adventure had only just begun. We were finally on safe ground although, as we later discovered, the road in front of us and behind us had been almost completely washed out. It was primarily fashioned from rather loose dirt anyway and was serving "temporarily" until the final version was built. We had arrived at least one construction phase too early as had all the company we encountered on the hillside. There were trucks filled with complaining pigs, millions of grapes from Turpan (the city's specialty crop) heading to the big city, and every which kind of packaged goods filling a variety of vehicles. However, there was no longer any way in or out of our place of salvation. We anticipated a long stay with our single bag of grapes and a couple of bottles of water we had purchased for the ride. It turned out that the young men from the van that rescued us were tourists from Eastern China and we kind of threw in our lot together. At one point they decided it would be more promising to hike over the substantial hills alongside the washed out roadway on which we were stranded to a nearby town and try to get on the train to Urumchi that ran there. We decided we would go along with that option as well. There did not seem to be any other, more promising one. They were kind enough to carry a few of the items we packed for the trek (we were forty-five years or so their seniors and that was one more act of kindness we experienced in the Third World). We started hiking along the remaining strip of road in front of us until we came to a place where we would need to climb a rather formidable hill to continue. A couple of our new Chinese companions went ahead to ascertain if it made sense for the entire group of us to start the climb. The report – there was no way through.

In disappointment, we headed back to our vehicles. Along the side of the road, we came across a few workers who resided there temporarily as members of a construction crew assigned to care for and upgrade the roadway. We purchased one of their live chickens and took it along with us. Together with the dozen young folks in the van, we then went about preparing for our evening's banquet. We secured a box of peaches from one of the trucks marooned alongside us and we were really rolling along preparing the evening's feast. I had bought a fancy Uygur knife in Kashgar in my pre-flood life. I handed it to our driver who did the chicken in and skillfully defeathered the bird. I suspected he was not born a driver but had put in many years on a farm. The van group found an old bucket on the floor of their vehicle and, though it had a small hole in it, managed to bring some water to a boil. Voila! Chicken in the bucket, peaches on a cloth and the banquet was about to begin.

That nibble or so of chicken, a drink from our water bottle and a sense of camaraderie brightened our prospects but we were quite aware that we were going to spend at least one night right where we were and probably more. As we surveyed the destruction around us after the water subsided, we imagined that even bringing water or food into the area would be a significant undertaking. We would more likely spend several hungry, thirsty, cool nights penned in where we were. When it got dark, we all got into our car to nestle down for the evening. We were serenaded by our next door animal friends complaining about the accommodations in the back of the crowded pig truck but even that failed to counter the total fatigue we had accumulated during the day. Everyone slept just fine even sitting upright and with little foot room in the old buggy.

The next day began with no more promise than the first had ended. There was no sign of help, not a vehicle had moved, and circumstances seemed even bleaker than the night before. The water had receded considerably but the road appeared totally impassable. We were even out of chicken. It was sometime in the early afternoon, as I was sitting in the shade of a nearby truck reading and protecting myself from the hot midday sun, that I spotted a cart carrying a tank of water entering our area. The local workers knew many folks were stranded and they had somehow gotten help through over existing narrow paths that had survived the flood. However, we were quite wary of water in that part of the world so our immediate situation did not improve. One could die from thirst or from drinking the water – tough choice. The workers who had brought the water became aware that, horror of horrors, there were two Americans stranded on the road along with the scores of Chinese about whom there was far less concern. Only a few hours went by before several men approached us. They had come from the main construction office a mile or so down the road. They motioned to us to follow them, packed up and carried our belongings and walked ahead on the narrow strip that was left of the road behind us. All around us we heard the sound of dynamite blasting a new temporary passage through the area so that vehicles could leave. We were quite hesitant about going with the men, not because we wanted to spend much more time where we were, but because we felt it was insulting and insensitive to their countrymen to worry just about us. And some of the ones left behind were our chicken partners. I guess the government was concerned about international publicity at the time (The year was 1996). Our guide insisted we go with the workers and promised everything would work out. We said goodbye to our new found friends, wished our driver and guide good luck and followed the workmen along the narrow strip that was left of the path behind us.

We shuffled along the path until we reached the construction office where we were soon transferred to a van and taken over a back road through the desert to the hotel we had left earlier in Turpan. It was no Hilton but it sure beat our last accommodation. The difficult task then was finding out what was happening to our driver and guide. We got no news that day but we did have food and water and a more comfortable place to lay our heads that night. About 24 hours after we arrived at the hotel, our driver and guide showed up, tired but looking none the worse than when we left them. A new, narrow, dirt roadway had been blasted out behind them and they were able to get out. We never found out when the rest of our fellow unfortunates escaped but we felt satisfied that they would all ultimately get to their respective destinations. There was no other way to get from Turpan to Urumchi we learned except for the train we were seeking at the town over the hills. We also discovered that the train we hoped to board had been washed out as well by the same storm and we would not have been able to travel on it had we managed to climb the formidable hills between us and that town and made our way to the junction.

Later on that night, the driver and I shared the wheel (he had little time to rest from his ordeal) and spent about five hours driving through the desert to the city of Dunhuang[1], home to the spectacular Thousand Buddha Caves, grottos decorated by monks and other devotees almost 1700 years ago. It was a traveler's highlight and a place I would love to have visited although it was not on our itinerary and the thought of being at the site of this remote cultural treasure was exciting while not being able to visit it was equally frustrating. The agency had arranged for us to be on a flight to Southern China at 5:00 that morning. No caves for us. We were lucky to get a few hours of rest after we arrived in Dunhuang. Our takeoff was at dawn. I doubt I will pass that way again. However interesting the area was, we were not unhappy to say goodbye to Xinjiang that morning.

Automobile Adventures

In the Third World, just driving along peacefully through the countryside can pose a challenge. Western China was not the only place where an automobile was at the center of strange events. In the northern area of the Cote D'Ivoire we were motoring toward our destination when another old car we were touring in began to stall. The motor soon stopped altogether. Our guide expressed worry about sitting immobilized in that sparsely inhabited part of the country but the driver was apparently cognizant of the presence of a mechanic in a town only a few miles up the road. Considering we had not passed any village for an hour or two that featured anything but mud huts, it was gratifying to receive that information. I do not know how the driver knew about the mechanic since he was not from that section of the country but he volunteered to hitch a ride from a passing car, get the mechanic to return with him and have the problem repaired. His optimism cheered us considerably and he left us to fulfill that mission.

We waited about an hour before our guide decided to try to restart the car and attempt to get closer to the town ahead. To our delight, he was successful in doing so. We started, drove about two hundred yards, stalled again, and repeated the process over and over until we actually reached the village where the mechanic supposedly practiced his trade. Sure enough, our driver was already there and had the mechanic in tow ready to return to where we had been stuck. That trip was no longer necessary so we had indeed saved a good bit of time. And we were in a more comfortable setting where water and food were available should we need them. The mechanic opened the hood, ascertained that the carburetor was not working properly because we had apparently gotten dirty gasoline somewhere along the way, took the carburetor out of the car, disassembled it completely, cleaned it off and put it back together and into the car once again. The key was turned and the motor ran smoothly once more. We were soon on our way. The whole operation cost about $6.00. Sorry that guy does not live near me. There is talent everywhere in the world but it is truly amazing to come across a mechanic in a remote village in northern Cote D'Ivoire who can diagnose and repair an automobile problem in less than an hour. Surprises abound in every aspect of our travels.

Another one of our exciting automobile trips took place one day in southern Mexico. We had been visiting the state of Chiapas and decided we would drive to Huatulco for a little resort relaxation in what we had heard was a beautiful Pacific coastal city. The drive was a relatively long one so we left fairly early in the day. The weather was lovely so we stopped at markets and in towns along the road and our voyage was leisurely and pleasant. It was only later that afternoon that we found ourselves on a relatively desolate stretch of road, just as the sun was setting and the darkness arriving. I had a notion that Huatulco was but an hour or two from where we were although it was hard to tell from the map I was using because we did not see any signs along the road that indicated where we were; the towns were simply too small to merit inclusion on my map. So we drove and we drove. It was not much longer before it turned quite dark and very lonely but the worst part of the experience was that our gasoline indicator showed that we were almost empty. My estimate of Huatulco being about a half hour away turned out to be grossly inaccurate.

When we finally encountered a young man walking along the road, I stopped and inquired about the distance to our destination. He told me that Huatulco was about one and a half or two hours from where we were. I doubted that he knew what he was talking about and assured Bev we were much nearer than that but I also asked about the availability of gasoline. He knew nothing about that. The day was getting late, we did not know where we were, we had no idea about where to secure more gas and Huatulco was an indeterminate distance from where we were. Oh, boy! Another one of those days. As it turned out, the person I asked was absolutely right. We rode along for well over an hour with the fuel indicator bobbing up and down near the empty mark. We did not find any place to purchase additional gasoline. We were riding on vapors and prayer but somehow we lucked out. Whatever I had in that tank sufficed. I do not know what I would have done were that not the case. My near misses kept adding up but we limped into a station on the outskirts of Huatulco and filled up like a thirsty elephant. We also had a nice couple of enjoyable days in that attractive Mexican resort.

Other drives were less dramatic but I have driven to dead ends in several isolated places including a most hostile looking village in the hills of Jamaica, a road that ended at the edge of a cliff in rural Mexico, and into the middle of demonstrations or police actions in several other carefully chosen locations. Of course, nothing ever came close to our China flood but no complaints about that here.

Whoops! My Fault.

Some of the more disconcerting experiences in my travels were occasions when I made a faux pas which offended an individual or a group of people who subsequently sought righteous vengeance upon me. Aside from the embarrassment and the disappointment in my judgment, I also had to get out of each situation post-haste. One such occasion took place in a Dogon village at the top of a high escarpment in Mali. There was a small market where I spotted a little girl sitting alone munching on a mango. Without thinking twice, I captured the scene rapidly with my camera. The girl's mother saw me do that and was outraged. She came over to me with her hands flailing and tried to hit me in the face. I was obviously unaware of possible objections to the picture taking (ugly American that I am) and I had not seen any adult near the girl. Fortunately, someone intervened as I was being attacked, I tried to sincerely apologize to little avail, and we finally all went on our way. Visitors need to know the rules about such things.

Two other such incidents came about while we were driving through lonely countrysides. On one such occasion somewhere in Sumatra, I spied a group of people walking along a path on a hill on the on other side of the road. They were dressed in rather traditional clothing and were headed to some ceremony or other. We did not stop to speak with them since they were a distance away but I again took out my camera to take a photo of the event from what I considered a reasonable space. Apparently, the group I was pointing my lens at did not agree. They responded quite angrily to my effort and several of the men rapidly descended the hill toward the road and our car. I did not think it was a propitious time to inquire about their business or intentions or to discuss my photography so I jumped back into the car and headed quickly out of there. I assume in retrospect that I had intruded into some solemn circumstance, perhaps a funeral parade or the like.

A third rather craven and dumb action on my part occurred in the Negev area of Israel. Some two hundred yards or so from the road where I was driving I saw a Bedouin village that looked colorful and busy. Although I was a distance from the houses, I again took out my long lens, fastened it on my camera and took a few pictures. About 100 feet behind me, I noticed an old car with several men inside pull up. They did not appear happy with my activity. I not only felt threatened but it was clear they were rushing toward me along the relatively isolated road I had taken. I quickly got back in the car and left there as quickly as I could. I am convinced that I was truly endangered, especially in the latter two instances. But even without any sense of threat, I try hard not to offend the people who live in places I visit. It is their home after all. They should set the standards and a traveler needs to be aware and respectful of their desires and sensitivities. Sometimes we mess up even with the best intentions.

Little Things Mean a Lot

Endless minor inconveniences along the paths we tread flood my memory but none of these turned any stretch of travel into a significantly negative experience. I think of the time in the mid-eighties when we were on a small ship on the Li River in China, a waterway that offers lovely scenery but not an inviting opportunity to swim. Bev turned to me after our on-board lunch and said, "I wonder where they wash the dishes and food." I surely had no idea until we came upon another tourist ship and saw for ourselves the system they used. There was a small platform on the back of the vessel and on it several kitchen workers were washing the dishes used by them for lunch – right in the Li River of course. Time for another laugh. What else can one do?

A week later, we visited Japan for a quite different experience. We did not worry about cleanliness in that country at all but our trip began with a taxi ride from the airport to our hotel. We made sure, we thought, that the driver was clear about where we were heading. We had a card with the name of the hotel in Japanese and English with us and showed it to the driver who took a quick look and said he knew the place. After a long drive, we arrived at the wrong hotel all the way on the opposite side of the city. The names were similar but one included the word "new" which he carelessly misread. After well over an hour, we arrived at the right place and were told the drive would cost $175.00. An argument ensued about who was responsible for the mistake and we agreed to settle for what the fare would have been had we taken the direct route. That was a good thing because it was the last stop for us at the end of a long journey and we were almost broke at the time.

It was no wonder that we had run out of money. Aside from all other costs, it was difficult to turn down some of the lovely objects we admired in Asia on our first trip there. It seemed that every country featured attractive, desirable folk creations that tempted us. Additionally, the merchants did not make it easy to turn down anything we peered at with interest. I remember at the beginning of our long Asian trip, we wandered through a store in Delhi. The object that caught our attention on that occasion was a carved, sandalwood statue of Krishna, the god who usually appears with a flute and a lovely woman[15]. The piece would have cost us virtually all of our budgeted shopping for the entire trip even though we did begin a bargaining process. We could not agree to a value in spite of the fact that the vendor came down considerably from his original asking price. We eventually decided not to buy the object and left for our hotel. This event occurred about midday. We decided to dine in our hotel that evening and, in the middle of our dinner, in came the salesperson with the Krishna statue to tell us he would let us have it for the amount we had indicated we would be willing to pay earlier in the day. Fortunately, as it turned out, we had changed our mind about the entire transaction by that time and told him we did not want the statue at all. He was disappointed of course but we were never sorry we skipped that transaction. Our trip had just begun and the purchase would have been a great mistake. We would have carried it the entire three months of the trip and would not have been able to purchase lovelier items that we encountered along the way.

One of the things we became more sophisticated and knowledgeable about in our Third World travel was shopping. And there is much to learn indeed. We found that guides, especially local ones we engaged from time to time to spend a day with us, would regularly stop at stores either upon request or on their own to have us shop in their presence. Sometimes those places were interesting and we could learn about the process of making something we considered artistic. What it took us a while to realize was

---

15   Krishna is the eighth incarnation of the Hindu God, Vishnu. He usually is depicted playing the flute. Krishna is the god of love and the frequently beautiful village maidens alongside him have been successfully seduced. While he also serves a protector of cows and sacred utterances, his primary purpose is to introduce the religion of love.

that the guide was given a substantial amount of the price of the object we bought. One instance brought home to us how much this is part of the system in many countries. We stopped at a jewelry store in Calcutta one day as we walked along with a guide. Bev admired a skillfully carved silver necklace which we would have been unlikely to afford in the States. We talked with the proprietor and found out what he would charge for it. As we bargained, our guide would simply not leave our presence. He had no prior arrangement with this store and we had entered it on our own. Yet, he engaged the owner in Bengali to insist that he get his usual cut for bringing tourists to shop. The owner resisted and we all left the store with no purchase. Later on that day, we returned by ourselves and bought the necklace without the approximately 25 per cent that would have gone to a guide who had done nothing to earn it. We no longer went to any stores with guides regardless of their urging.

Another occasional annoyance for us in our travels was Bev's pet peeve which had to do with overnight train rides in India. Traveling in a sleeper car rather than flying from place to place has several advantages including meeting people, seeing the countryside and saving money. Sometimes, it is the only practical connection between towns. There is one problem however. Compartments in First Class sleep four and in Second Class they frequently sleep eight. We customarily splurge on First Class train travel which most folks I know would not consider very luxurious. Yet that also usually means sleeping with two strangers. We tend to be on the train a little more promptly than local first class passengers and so we organize ourselves and sit in the compartment until the train pulls out. Bev tends to get more and more optimistic as we approach the departure time of the train. Each time, however, her hopes are dashed by the arrival of fellow travelers, pretty much always men. She has spent more time sleeping alongside three men than any other woman I know.

There are always challenges, small and large, to surmount in Third World travel and the ones cited above are but a few of our memorable ones. We have climbed awkward cutout logs to get into traditional buildings 15 feet or more feet above ground or onto moored vessels, we have crossed rope bridges to reach some desired destination, we have gotten lost on empty roads or seen our gas indicator at near empty where there was no apparent source of gasoline, we have found ourselves in the midst of dark gatherings of angry people, we have been attacked by cockroaches or mosquitoes and we have breathed deeply at each escape. Yet we have never regretted being some place or other or doing what we did. (Well, almost never.) It was always part of our ongoing journey. I do not seek such risky adventure but precarious escapades sometimes come with the territory. Adventure never arrives without the shadow of peril walking nearby.

Roadside in Sikkim, northeastern India

Tribal people carrying goods to the market in Orissa

Valle de la Luna (Valley of the Sun) near La Paz, Bolivia

Young monk in training, Tibetan temple

CHAPTER FIVE

BIG PILLS, LITTLE PILLS

"If you reject the food, ignore the customs, fear the religion and avoid the people, you might better stay at home."

— James Michener

So what happens if you do get sick? That is unquestionably the most common worry expressed by people I interact with or lecture to about places I have gone or by my friends or others contemplating the possibility of following in my tracks. Matters relating to cleanliness and health are the most anxiety producing concerns folks express about what may happen on a trip, although I suspect it is uncertainty about what unexpected challenges they might encounter that is the larger demon lying at the heart of people's resistance to travel in the Third World. As I mentioned earlier, we have been extremely fortunate with our health. Except for a couple of encounters south of the border with traveler's stomach, Bev has done quite well. As for me, I have had only a couple of bad experiences in a lifetime of travel although they were lollapaloozas. When people ask me about medical facilities in casual conversations, I usually reply that there are shamans and witch doctors everywhere I travel and they actually make house calls if necessary.

There is an element of truth to that although it is a facetious answer. I appreciate Western medicine as much as anyone else accustomed to it.

Shaking the Bed

I have to go back to my very first journey outside the States to recall the only significant illness I ever contracted outside the country, namely, bacterial dysentery. I mentioned earlier the fact that I had been teaching for a year by the summer of 1955 and had saved enough money to drive to Mexico with a colleague at my school who had bought a new, shiny, reliable Pontiac. We motored cross country and ultimately stayed most of the summer in a boarding house in Mexico City. The trip was quite an eye-opener. It turned out to be an experience which greatly encouraged my future travel. That is, all except for the consequences of one side trip to Acapulco. I knew enough to avoid the local water in Mexico but somehow foolishly drank milk at a small restaurant in the run-down part of town that weekend.

By the time we returned to Mexico City, I was not feeling very well. The next morning, I had a raging fever and chills. My bed in the boarding house was a large four poster and it and I rocked together frequently and forcefully that day. I felt like I was dying. A fellow boarder was a first year medical student in the city from Panama so he knew exactly what was happening to me: I had malaria. He pronounced his diagnosis authoritatively as he stood by the side of my bed; no one even thought to challenge him. I took my aspirins, drank my water and observed my body temperature rising and falling. As it turned out, I did not have malaria at all but just an acute, virulent case of dysentery. I don't know if my fellow boarder ever graduated from his medical studies but two days later my fever left me. I was weak for much of the rest of the trip, but I had survived and would go on to finish my ambitious journey. We headed from Mexico City to California and then back across the country to my home in Philadelphia.

I was not the same person for a couple of weeks after that episode and did not regain my full strength until about the time I arrived home, yet I found myself inconvenienced but unscarred by the experience. The trip had been life changing in other ways and my illness and recovery were only a small part of its totality. I never shied away from such travel after that time because of general apprehension until my body developed some very special needs later on in my life. There were no negative physical or psychological after effects to that interlude.

Burmese Medicine

The next seemingly significant medical issue I encountered occurred some 32 years later. During a three month long trip through Asia, we made a stop in Burma. At the time, that poor, long suffering country was even more isolated than it is today. The lack of any real tourist infrastructure or any apparent desire on the part of the government to create one was another impediment to travel. One see med able to count the visitors by the dozens. We foreigners were curiosities wherever we went. It appeared that there was only one international flight that flew in and out of the international airport each day and one internal plane (Could it have been the same one?) that made a round of four cities within the country. The roads outside of Mandalay and Rangoon were dirt covered and people in the countryside rode horse or water buffalo drawn carts or heavy bicycles. Visitors were permitted only seven day visas so you needed to move along briskly if you wanted to see much of the place. Even then, the people running things apparently did not want visitors poking around and discovering facts about their homeland.

Reservations for sleeping were quite scarce because there were few hotels and all of the existing ones left much to be desired. It was almost impossible to change any reservation that was already prearranged so one needed a lot of luck to survive spontaneous or independent travel (bribery was the only potential alternative to the absence of a hotel accommodation). We did try to move along without prior arrangements but without a lot of success. Additionally, big brother seemed to be everywhere and was always watching interactions between Burmese and tourists. Over 20 years later as I write these lines, big brother is still there, and in an even less benign and decidedly more threatening posture.

That was the setting for my emergency medical experience. The occurrence started in the little town of Pagan (now renamed Bagan by the ruling Junta), a must stop on the Burma tourist route. Bagan features a plethora of temples, each a thousand years or so old, scattered over a large plain with the Irrawaddy River in the background. When we visited there the first time, the preferred mode of transportation even for tourists was a horse cart- flat, hard and very bumpy. I did not notice anything unusual during our ride to see the important temples but the next morning, as I prepared to leave our hotel, I felt a little twitch in my abdomen. I decided there was nothing to be concerned about and continued my activities as I normally would. We rushed to collect our bags and boarded an open truck which was to carry about twenty of us tourists to the airport. Not long after we were along the way, Bev asked me if I had the passports. A quick check alerted me to the fact that they were not with us (I always carry them in my fanny pack which I was wearing.) We were only a few minutes from the hotel so I immediately banged on the back window of the cab of our vehicle to ask the driver to turn around so we could retrieve them. He motioned that he would do so but obviously did not understand a single word I said. As a brief panic began to penetrate my consciousness, I banged several times more. It was clear we were not going back with him. We remembered there was only one flight that day and there was no room available in Pagan that night. We needed to be in Rangoon a couple of days later to be able to get home on the day our flight out of the country was scheduled.

Heroes

We arrived at the airport about a half hour later after I gave up on the driver and roughly thirty minutes before our flight was to depart. Our traveling companions were all familiar to us; most of us had shared a train ride to Mandalay earlier (due to the fact that we could not get any flights) and we were among the few tourists in Burma. Even that train ride was memorable in that it was about 90° inside the train that evening when the windows were closed. Since the Water Festival was in process, every time we came into a station, we had to quickly shut all the windows so we did not get soaked by the festival celebrants of the towns we passed through. It was hard to know if the heat in the train or the water thrown at us in the stations was more dangerous. We were awake throughout most of the night laughing hysterically as we cooperated in the water watch. One person or other yelled "station" when an upcoming stop was sighted and the rest of us slammed our windows shut until we left the platform five or ten minutes later. It was a very bonding experience. At any rate, most of us kept bumping into each other all over Burma afterward as we all wound up visiting the same places at about the same time. Our traveling comrades immediately indicated their empathy for our passport dilemma and promised the plane would not take off without us. I ran around desperately outside the airport entrance trying to find a ride back to the hotel. Finally, another truck driver agreed to take me to the hotel and back for a reasonable fee and I was off. The passports as well as all the vouchers for the remainder of the extensive Asia trip we had barely begun had fallen behind a shelf in the closet of our hotel room. I enthusiastically grabbed them and ran to the truck. I arrived back at the airport over an hour after we had left it and the sight was extremely heartwarming and welcome. The plane had indeed arrived and was waiting to take off. Some fellow tourists were sitting on the tarmac in front of the plane; others were standing in the doorway of the cabin and otherwise preventing it from leaving. Bev was frantically waving to me to hurry up. We had all found a cause. I was most grateful for everyone's participation and ran as quickly as I could toward the open door. Mission accomplished. Yet there turned out to be one slight hitch.

After I thanked the others on the plane profusely for their heroic effort, I sank into my seat sweaty and drained. Too much running around in the Burma heat. By the time we arrived in Rangoon, I became aware of a sharp pain developing in my abdomen. When we finally reached our room in the hotel, I collapsed into bed with a level of pain I had never experienced before. For just the second time in all my travels, I clearly needed a doctor. Coincidentally, back in Mandalay, a few days earlier, I had exchanged stories with another American tourist and, as it turned out, received what was to be unexpectedly valuable information from him. He elaborated on the backward state of medicine in the country. In the process he also told us about Dr. Bob who worked at the U.S. embassy in Rangoon and who would occasionally offer his services to touring Americans in distress although he was actually there to attend to embassy personnel. My new acquaintance had met Dr. Bob and had occasion to use his skills. I did not foresee the import of that conversation during my next few days of travel in Burma but the information was to come in very handy when we reached Rangoon.

Lost Body

I told Bev to call the embassy and ask if the doctor we heard about earlier in our trip would see me. My pain seemed to be increasing by the minute. She was informed that the doctor was out on the golf course and could not be reached (It was Wednesday in Burma so why would he be available?) His wife answered the phone and said he would call me back. I did not know when I would hear from him. I just knew I hurt a lot. As a matter of fact, I was so desperate that I had Bev go down to the desk and ask them to call a Burmese doctor. You cannot get much more desperate than that. Medicine in Burma in the 1980's was reputed to be equivalent to the level of ours sometime in the 1920's. At that time, Burmese students had little opportunity to travel to the United States or to Europe for their medical education and then return to practice in their own country in contrast to the situation in many other places in Asia.

The Burmese doctor arrived in an hour or so with his longyi[16] flapping. He looked about the age of our daughter who was roughly twenty at the time and he was closely followed by a nurse carrying a bag with a red cross on it. Heaven knows what was inside that container. As I agonized in my room, Bev led him in and introduced him. A brief examination took place; the diagnosis - an abdominal

---

16   The Myanmar "longyi," is a sarong-like garment and the most notable part of the Myanmar national dress worn by men as well as women. It is a piece of cloth sown into a cylindrical tube, slipped over the head by men and stepped into by the women. It is then tucked in at the waist. Men and women fasten longyis at the waist in different ways. Men fold the garment into two panels and knot it neatly at waist level. Women use it as a wrap-around skirt and tuck it in on the side.

strain. Oh, goodness, what kind of strain could that be? At any rate, he was the only medical person I had consulted; he made the diagnosis and then presented me with a pill that seemed about the size of a ping pong ball. I did what any reasonable, suffering, panicked person would do. I took it. I did not trust the diagnosis or the pill one bit but at least it was treatment.

The pain did not diminish at all. As a matter of fact. It seemed to get worse. An hour or so later, the embassy doctor called and said I was welcome to come on over. Somehow, I struggled outside, into a taxi, and finally to the embassy. The doctor's wife let us in and asked us to sit down in the parlor. Bev happened to see a note on the doctor's desk that had been written to him after my call. It read: "A Mr. Diamond called to see you. He has a problem and needs your help. He says he saw a Burmese doctor, ha, ha, ha." Ha, ha, ha indeed. The new diagnosis after Dr. Bob examined me was that I was suffering from a probable kidney stone. The worrisome quandary was his assertion that there was no way to get acceptable treatment for that in Burma. "We need to get you out of the country as soon as possible," the doctor said. "I am sending you to a clinic in Rangoon today and we will try to get you on tomorrow's plane. I want you to check into a hospital in Bangkok as soon as you arrive. I will make the arrangements." Nothing like hearing a diagnosis that could not be treated in Burma and requiring a flight for which I had no tickets as well as having to spend a night in a mosquito collecting center called a clinic in Rangoon. That was one of the very few moments of travel when I would have preferred to be home.

The next chapter of this experience went far better than the first, at least for me. My pain actually diminished slightly. Bev was able to get into town by taxi to acquire the bottles of water I was told to drink that night. She bravely did so in spite of the fact that it was still Water Festival time in Burma resulting in people pouring water on her head and down her back as she walked along the street. As if that were not enough aggravation, the scariest aspect of the whole affair for Bev was that she failed to note where the clinic was located or what its name was when she left for the center of the city. She actually got into the taxi and rode away without knowing where she was coming from. After realizing that fact, she spent the ride shouting at the non-English speaking driver that she did not know where the clinic was. To no avail. It was a repeat of our experience with the truck driver who took us to the airport. That was the first time she completely lost me in our travels although she was prone to getting lost herself. Since I was unaware that I was lost, I was not at all discomforted by the circumstance but she was terrified. The doctor who treated me at the clinic suggested that Bev get a couple of bottles of water for me to drink so that I could pass the kidney stone he suspected I had and she was also en route to get our new tickets from the airline. Along the way, Bev met up with our fellow travelers who had held up the plane for us. They were upset when she related the story about my pain and subsequent diagnosis. When she finally reached the airline office, she met with a prominent orthopedist Dr, Bob had contacted for us. He was willing to use his influence to get us new tickets out of the country. Bev explained that she had lost me because she had no idea what the clinic was called nor where it was. Luckily, he was familiar with the location where my lost body lay so Bev was able to make her way back to me. Incidentally, we have been in contact with that orthopedist ever since and had dinner at his house on our subsequent visit to the country but that is a totally different story. Bev returned to the clinic exhausted and dripping wet from the festival celebrants who were enjoying themselves pouring water down her blouse and on her head even as she lugged several bottles of water along the sidewalk to flush my

133

kidney stones. It was not her best day but she did manage all the tasks necessary. The next morning we could not even get a taxi to take us to the airport and we wound up riding in an ambulance because revelers had hired all the taxis available that day. While we rode along the busy streets, we were nonetheless regular recipients of water tossed our way. The red cross on our vehicle was apparently mistaken for a target. Oh, well, off to Bangkok, then to Samitivey Hospital, an elegant private facility which featured several American trained interns, quite comfortable rooms, modern equipment and nurses who actually answered calls graciously though they could not speak a word of English. I stayed there five days (for just a couple of hundred dollars) in a room with a bed for Bev, a refrigerator filled with delicacies, and at least one comprehensive X-ray study each day. The upshot was that the Burmese doctor had been right all along. They found no kidney stone. My pain had left me entirely by the third or fourth day at Samitivey. The problem turned out to be a strain, they explained, probably incurred on the horse cart. Nothing showed up on the X-rays at all and the worst that happened was that we missed a couple of days touring Thailand. What do I do about medical problems? There you have it! I wonder what that pill was anyway. There were no witch doctors available on the one occasion I could have used one but I think I came close.

As I mentioned elsewhere, Bev and I do bring along some drugs for self-medication and they come in handy from time to time. We tend to need them occasionally for stomach illness which one can contract practically everywhere we go, probably because things are not sufficiently sanitary or properly refrigerated but also as a result of the fact that we are just not used to the food or water. We try to be careful and, as I said earlier, we have been extremely lucky in respect to health. Bev has had occasional tummy trouble, especially in Mexico and once in a while in India or Southeast Asia, but I have escaped even that for the most part. We also sometimes use Pepto-Bismol tablets prophylactically in places where we know the food is less than reliable. Of course, we do miss out on some culinary treats by being cautious, especially by avoiding eating from street vendor stands, but that is the ever-present tourist trade-off. If one does become ill, the days spent in bed are lost travel time. At the same time, the more careful one is, the more one misses. This is true for all aspects of the travel experience. Of course, foolhardiness is an invitation to catastrophe and we do want to maximize our time enjoying the places we journey to.

The Big Bang

My most recent problematic incident occurred during a family trip to South Africa. The event could not be blamed on Third World medical facilities since South Africa is a place where quite good health services are available. The injury I sustained could actually have happened anywhere including at home. My balance has not been wonderful the last year or so due to both age and illness and, as I was getting into the passenger seat of our van to leave the site of the safari camp we had stayed at for the previous several days, I turned to get something behind me and somehow slipped off the seat backwards and fell about four feet to the ground. I landed flat on my back and I knew right away that I had broken several ribs. I decided there was no point going to a doctor since broken ribs are normally untreatable. I did not even bother with an X-ray. We were only four days into our twelve day sojourn so substantial pain accompanied me the rest of the time. I did manage to survive those eight days with the help of pain pills and lidocaine patches and I was able to enjoy much of the remaining time we traveled in spite of my injury. Interestingly, I had only taken those pain preventatives with me on the trip because of a medical procedure I had a week before the trip. Bringing pain pills was a fortunate instance of payoff for my being atypically careful. I would normally not have had the medication or the patches with me. Ah, serendipity!

Even with Technology

I should mention here one other medical emergency I was present for although I was not the victim in that instance. Once while traveling with another couple, there was an incident which became an indirect medical experience for us. The four of us were traveling in Costa Rica, one of the more prosperous and well developed nations south of our border where we were luxuriating on a beautiful beach. All of a sudden, I saw my buddy fall in rather shallow water and noticed that he was unable to lift himself up. With the help of another nearby tourist I managed to help him (perhaps drag him is a better term) out of the water entirely and onto the sand. It turned out that he had significantly torn up his knee by getting caught in an undertow and twisting it in an unusual position. I was later to learn he had actually destroyed a couple of ligaments and rendered his knee rather useless. What were we to do? There was no lifeguard on duty but I did locate a helpful park attendant. With his assistance we secured a wheelbarrow (the only transportation available), put my friend into it and managed to wheel him out of the park to our rental car where he crawled into the back seat in great pain. I suspected our trip was heading toward a rather fast ending at that point.

The next challenge was securing medical care. Fortunately, I was able to find local folks at the beach who directed me to a public health clinic only a few miles away. Now public health clinics in the Third World are wonderful innovations and have served and comforted innumerable people but they are not the most desirable sites for fussy

American tourists to patronize nor are they locations for the most contemporary and comprehensive health care. We found the place we were directed to at the end of a dirt road overlooking a beautiful panorama of sea and coastline and managed to get my friend inside.

It was apparent to all of us including the medic in the clinic that the knee was badly damaged and needed surgery and my friend made clear that no surgery was to take place on his knee in Costa Rica (We surely were not going to arrange for it at that clinic). The challenge was to immobilize the knee, get our patient onto a plane home and have him check in with an orthopedic surgeon. A full leg cast was needed to minimize pain and prevent further damage to the knee and the medic prepared the material for a cast and was ready to put it on. Two issues arose. One had to do with the intense pain that my friend was suffering and the other was the leg itself. He refused anything that would have to be injected to ease the pain because he did not trust the needles in the clinic. His caution was probably due to his knowledge about infection from his background as a veterinarian. The setting did not invite much trust on our part as to sanitary procedures so I well understood his reluctance to be injected there. Thus he suffered much more than he would have at home. (I have carried a hypodermic needle with me on several trips ever since). The leg cast was ready and the medic prepared to put it on—right on top of the sand that was sticking to the entire lower part of my friend's body. What a great idea! My Spanish came in very handy at that moment. I succeeded in making him understand that the cast might be on there for a day or two and a layer of sand would unquestionably irritate his skin and make his discomfort even greater. The leg was cleaned off, the cast was placed on it, and my friend managed to arrange a helicopter ride to San Jose where a flight to the States was scheduled for the next day.

Bev and I drove our rental car back to San Jose the following day anticipating that our traveling companions were already well out of the country. As we entered the hotel sometime after lunch, our friend greeted us with the news that he could not get a flight out until that evening. We met him in the lobby sitting on a chair mounted on a porter's clothes carrier holding his crutches with his full leg cast on display. He looked like some cartoon version of a tribal king in some exotic country. When we saw that apparition approaching us, we burst out into uncontrollable laughter. That just goes to show you that even the direst of incidents can have a comical side. I will never forget that picture and we still refer to it with amusement from time to time when we are together. The Third World surely is full of surprises. My friend finally got home and took care of the problem although he has been rather reluctant to travel to a number of places I have suggested since that event took place. Could that have happened anywhere? Probably but it is more likely to result in the experiences I have cited in the places I go.

For those for whom medical issues are a concern, I recommend that insurance to cover healthcare expenses and medical evacuation be purchased before a trip to any area where there is a dearth of decent medical facilities. A search for travel insurance on the internet will yield many options and there are sites which offer comparative features and prices. For most healthy people, the cost of insurance is probably not worth the expense. If you already have a medical condition you are worried about traveling with, pay for the insurance within a specified time after you have put money down on reservations and most companies will cover you for problems you incur on the trip caused by a preexisting condition.

It is worth mentioning in the context of medical issues, however, that there are some strange and potent diseases one might encounter in travel to some of the places I mention in this book. We have far fewer problems with communicable diseases and water-borne medical problems in the United States and most of the industrialized world. Yellow fever, poliomyelitis, cholera, many parasitic agents, dengue fever, and especially malaria are all comparatively rare in our part of the world. One should check world health sites so that concentrations of these problems can be avoided or at least intelligently minimized. For example I take pills for malaria prevention if I am planning to spend time in places where the disease is prevalent. There is no reason to take chances with exotic health risks although sometimes one must simply choose between taking a gamble or not going to a particularly hazardous place. Not every disease has a prophylactic treatment of medicine or vaccine. Again, great care in drinking and eating or covering skin at vulnerable times may be the best preventative. Mosquitoes seem to be the traveler's as well as residents' greatest threat. Their prevalence is often related to the seasonal rainfall in a particular area which can also be ascertained in guide books or on the internet. In the United States, the Center for Disease Control and Prevention has an excellent web site with information about recommended health precautions for travelers at http://wwwn.cdc.gov/travel. *If you are headed to places where cholera or malaria or other such diseases exist, a visit to a local travel health clinic is highly advised.*

If you have no handicap or disease to worry about when you travel, consider preparing for and braving the risks and head for the Third World in spite of any hesitation about potential medical problems. I think you will appreciate that advice if you heed it. The best time to take care of medical problems is before you leave. Vaccinations should be updated, medicines and other health supplies packed in your luggage, and common sense practices about cleanliness and other risk factors attended to along the way. *Hand cleanliness is one important step a traveler can take to fend off communicable diseases. Wipes and antiseptic liquids are essential. Soap and hot water are often absent in third world restaurant settings. And do not neglect open sores or cuts which might not merit your attention at home. Clean them up and use anti-bacterial creams. It is far easier for infections to develop during travel.* The traveler who does all he can to avoid problems is probably in no more danger than someone crossing the street in a busy American city or peddling a bicycle down a park side hill. And make sure not to walk casually through high crime areas of London or New York or LA or Amsterdam at 3:00 in the morning before you go on your trip. You may lose your deposit.

CHAPTER 6

JUST HAVING FUN

Unchecked, the tourist will climb over the fence and come right into your house to take pictures of you in your habitat. Cities mindful of tourists have built elaborate "tourist traps" which, luckily, work. Tourists are kept confined to these, and few escape. There is, of course, the type known as the "intrepid tourist." This one has to be watched carefully or he can become most annoying. Little wonder these are so often the target of terrorists. If there is an aspect of benign terror about the tourist, there is also a great deal of tourist in the terrorist. Terrorists travel with only one thing in mind, just like the tourist, and the specifics of places escape them both. Terrorists travel for the purpose of shooting unsuspecting foreigners, just as tourists travel for the purpose of shooting them with a camera.
—Andrei Codrescu (b. 1947), Romanian-born poet, radio commentator. "The Tourist"

Unless you have fun along the way, travel is something neither you nor I would be interested in pursuing. Of course, the experiences I called highlights earlier transcend what we would call just fun and the scariest, most threatening

141

moments one encounters can produce a high level of anxiety and discomfort, yet most of the things we wind up doing on our travel vacations are just entertaining and pleasurable. If they are not, we are probably in the wrong place undertaking the wrong activity. The truth is, however, that Third World travel also promises us longer lasting pleasure and memories and personal change opportunity than lolling about on a beach or indulging ourselves at a self contained resort are likely to offer.

So many recollections of moments of pure delight during travel crowd my memory that I could never list them all here so I will just share a few to illustrate what I mean by travel fun. Instances of these took place in Southeast Asia when we rented motorbikes (as I did in earlier travels in other places) to get about in Vientiane in Laos and Danang in Vietnam. The day we arrived in the quiet capital city of Laos, the weather was calm and sunny, perfect for walking along comfortably among the Wats or temples the city offers the traveler. It was no problem that day to amble around and sample the markets and religious sites of the 80,000 or so people who live there. To access the colorful countryside the next day however, we decided to rent a moped so we could cover more miles and sample some of the many villages in the outlying area; we would roll along on two wheels much as the typical resident does there. We found moped rental to be quite available in the city. After skirting successfully around the area during most of the day, we parked the vehicle at our hotel when we went to bed that evening looking forward to the next day's touring. When we awoke the following morning, rain had arrived. My inclination was to return our rental to the company we had secured it from and get around on foot or by taxi. Bev looked about at the many mopeds (the most common transportation for the residents of the city) making their way through the rain that morning, most of which carried two people (or sometimes an entire family); one of the passengers typically sat behind the driver holding up an umbrella. She said, "If the Laotians are managing to do that, we can too." That was all the encouragement I needed. We spent most of the next ten hours or so riding all over in our vehicle with Bev holding an umbrella over our heads as effectively as she could and me driving and splashing along the main streets. We did get to see most of the city though we were a bit soaked from the downpour by the time we finished. It turned out to be a great day of the kind of fun I am referring to. We laughed together most of the time and we surely did not waste a single hour that day cooped up in our hotel. It was also an experience that we recall often to share one more chuckle about.

The second moped experience that I recall here was even more fun. We had a bit of extra time in Danang, a city on the coast of Vietnam and decided to go on a little adventure. We rented our bike and took a ride to the interesting town of Hoi An, a locale settled as a commercial center by Chinese from Fujian across the bay in the 16th and 17th centuries. It is a walkable city with many old houses and temples where quite a few of the descendants of those maritime settlers still live or pray while they often retain many of their cultural practices. The city somehow did not find its way onto our itinerary as was the case with many other places we discovered willy-nilly so this was a special opportunity. Since we had no plans that day and had arranged no transportation, a moped was as good a way to go as any. I suggested we rent two and each of us drive our own, but Bev immediately turned down that idea and decided she would ride on the back of mine. I secured directions from the hotel concierge, rented the vehicle and left after lunch. On the road we took there were few cars as is usually the case in that part of Vietnam, but we sure did encounter lots of people walking and a multitude on bicycles and other mopeds. It turned out that the road we took was under serious repair most of the way. Of course, we could not read the signs at all so we never knew quite where we were, nor could we communicate with the other travelers as virtually no English was spoken along that road. We drove and drove but saw no indication that we were any closer to Hoi An. Luckily another moped driver hailed us in English after he apparently noticed that we were a bit confused. We learned from him that we had taken the wrong road to begin with and would never get to Hoi An by going straight. Fortunately, as is the case almost everywhere we have ventured in our travels and especially in every corner of Vietnam, the man was friendly, helpful and sympathetic. He said he was going in the general direction of Hoi An and beckoned us to follow him. At the point where he turned away onto another road, he explained how we should continue and, thanks to his generous help, we actually did get to Hoi An that day, albeit an hour or so later than we had hoped.

We ultimately had a fine afternoon finding our way through the town, visiting the highlights, stopping at the market and eventually discovering the right road back to Danang. The problem we then faced was that it grew dark as we neared Danang and we learned that the assorted bicycles, carts, and mopeds that became ever more numerous along the road as we neared the city were either not equipped with lights or had decided not to use those they had. The streets in town had almost no illumination at all. Oh, well, Danang in the dark with but a few inches between us and the next vehicle - another challenge. It was one more instance of unplanned intimacy. We finally made our way to the hotel without incident and returned the moped the next day.

Scary Underwater Fun

Scuba diving always appeared to us to be fun also. Unfortunately, we have never taken a course in that sport so our likelihood of ever diving was not a part of our planning. When we sailed in the South Pacific to the narrow island of New Britain, a beautiful locale that is part of Papua New Guinea, it was primarily to experience the snorkeling on the great reef which winds its way up from just off the Australian East Coast. We went to a resort there which we learned was apparently quite famous among divers as one of the great places in the world to explore underwater life. There were other attractions that drew us to the island, but the water and the beauty of the reef were the primary ones. After an afternoon drive through the area and a visit to several sites that were significant during World War II during our battle to drive the Japanese from the South Pacific, we arranged to go out on a diving boat the next morning with our snorkeling equipment.

We awoke excited about the day ahead of us, devoured a hearty breakfast with the divers who had come there from all over the globe, and got into our boat with about a dozen of them. At a certain point, the boat stopped and the divers jumped into the deep with their tanks and masks for a special treat. We watched enviously and prepared to be taken to our nearby snorkeling site. The underwater life we witnessed on that excursion enchanted us. The fish and coral that appeared underneath us were probably more diverse than just about anywhere else we have snorkeled. After we finished that activity, the instructor who was in our boat with us asked if we would like to dive. We informed him that we had never taken a single minute of instruction and preferred not to drown that day in the South Pacific waters no matter how inviting the setting seemed. He explained that there was not much for us to learn because he intended to personally accompany us into the deep. The offer was just too tempting and titillating to refuse. He gave us about fifteen minutes of instruction and said he would manage our equipment. No schooling necessary, no diving license to produce, no worries at all. This was New Britain, not our local pool. We decided that it was the opportunity of a lifetime and that we would not pass it up. As a long time snorkeler, I was always a bit envious of folks diving in the waters nearby.

In his lecture, the instructor demonstrated how to put the tank and mask on and how to proceed into the water. He went over some basics like the speed of descending and rising up, gave us a few signals to let him know how things were going, dressed us up for the occasion and led the way down the ladder into the water. One of our instructions was about how to clear the mask properly should water get inside. The failure to follow that instruction turned out to be my downfall. As we descended, I felt water slowly seeping into my mask and tried to follow our leader's directions about emptying it. Instead I allowed much more water inside. By the time we reached what was about a 20-foot submersion to the bottom, my mask felt full and I felt panicky. Bev had done well but I had not. I motioned to him with the signal he told us to use if we were in trouble and wanted to go up. He was disappointed, Bev was incredulous, and I was scared. He motioned to her to hold onto a rock that was right near us while he escorted me back into the ship. I climbed the ladder nervously, hoping to avoid the kind of problems one can incur from going too fast as he closely followed me to the surface. When I was back in the boat and had managed to separate myself from the tank, the instructor hustled back into the water and he and Bev spent at least 20 minutes down there without me. She sat there holding on to the designated rock anticipating that she would never see the instructor or the boat again but she still managed to turn around and look at the coral which surrounded her. Why waste time – especially if you are about to die? Because of her nervousness, her oxygen was depleting more quickly than it would have otherwise. By the time the instructor returned, she had used up much of the tankful which limited the time she had for underwater exploration. Nonetheless, as worried as she was about my predicament, she bravely roamed the area alongside her guide for one of the thrills of her life. Even more impressive is the fact that she is afraid of water and does not know how to swim. She is remarkable in her willingness to face her fears and limitations. I was the one back in the boat, somewhat embarrassed and quite disappointed.

As things turned out, I went back into the water with the instructor later on and was able to take pleasure in viewing the reef sharks and rays that Bev had been swimming with earlier. I had obviously not followed the guidelines about clearing my mask properly when I first got in the water which cost me the first part of our outing and made me feel like a real dummy. It was heavenly back in the deep especially since I had also conquered my mask filling problem to an extent that left me far more content than I was on the first try. Neither of us ever took further lessons to become certified divers but we both experienced some of the joy that I assume is a regular part of that endeavor. I am quite certain that scary fun is even more exciting and rewarding than just plain vanilla fun. It was for us. We have never again visited as inviting a dive site as the one we discovered in New Britain.

The Market in the Desert

Timbuktu, sitting at the edge of the great Sahara Desert, is one of the most romantic destinations the traveler can aspire to visit. What makes it so is that, in addition to its history as a famous center of Islamic study and a crossroads and market for the many caravans that plied the Western Sahara, it was a place which Westerners were banned from entering for centuries. What was at one time a thriving city of over 100,000 people is now a town of fewer than 15,000 residents which is slowly being swallowed by the advancing sands. The populace includes primarily Tuareg[17] people whose ancestors manned the ancient market stalls and drove the caravans across the mighty desert generations ago in the then thriving salt and gold trade. The afternoon we were to take a camel ride into the desert did not begin with a clear promise of fun. The temperature in mid-day topped 105^0. I sat on a hill overlooking the old city talking with a few people who were taking advantage of a light breeze outside in the shade and I joined them in swatting away the multitude of flies that decided to keep us company that afternoon. Bev was back in the room of our alleged hotel alternately soaking herself in the cold water shower in our room and sitting on a towel on the floor reading until she dried off. She repeated this process many times until the sun began to lower in the sky. Obviously, the actual enjoyment was to arrive a bit later.

And indeed it did! At about 4:00, we met our Tuareg guide with the unlikely name of Mohammed Ali. He was dressed in the typical blue shaded, flowing and loose fitting

---

17   The Tuaregs are a Caucasian ethnic group whose presence was first recorded over 2000 years ago along the Mediterranean. Until trucks and other European vehicles took over in the 20th century, they drove caravans from the Mediterranean Sea all the way into what is now Mali and Burkina Faso. They most often carried compact items of a luxury nature. The Tuareg are a fairly numerous diverse group of non-Arabic, Muslim people who share a common language and a common history. Tuareg camel caravans played the primary role in trans-Saharan trade until the mid-20th century. Later on European trains and trucks took over the route. Goods that Tuaregs once brought north from the edge of the Sahara no longer need their caravan service. Many Tuaregs have slowly moved southward in response to pressures from the North and the promise of a more prosperous land in the South. Tuaregs usually live in sedentary communities in cities bordering the Sahara that once were centers of trade for western Africa.

outfit the tribal group traditionally wears and he sported a scarf which covered his head and whose opening was configured so that only his nose and eyes would be exposed to the sand that can blow so strongly in the desert. He was a handsome man; we found the Tuaregs to be very attractive people for the most part. Mohammed greeted us accompanied by two camels and two camel boys. We mounted those remarkably uncomfortable animals and began to make our way out of town. If you have never ridden a camel, you cannot truly appreciate the efforts of those who traveled in caravans for weeks under the fiery sun that bakes the sands of the Sahara and other such routes in the deserts of the world. One mounts a camel as the animal sits on the ground with its legs drawn up under it, somewhat like you might picture a household cat. That is not too difficult to manage especially if there is a saddle with a post to grab onto. After the rider has mounted, the camel rises up, back legs first. You immediately feel that you are about to be tossed right off the front of the animal at that point. Then the forelegs go up and you feel that you are about to be thrown off backwards. If you remain on the camel's back, precariously gripping the post on the saddle for balance, the camel may turn around to take a look at you. They have occasionally been known to spit at unwelcome riders. All in all, a camel ride becomes an unnerving but precious experience that is a lot of fun. We have done this a number of times and found humor in the effort each time. But this adventure had just begun.

We headed off slowly as the sun began to sink into the horizon in front of us and as the temperature finally dipped to a tolerable level. With Mohammed Ali leading the way, the camel boys walked alongside their animals holding onto the straps and we sat mounted on our stately beasts as our caravan proceeded into Tuareg land. There were a few scrawny bushes along the way offering occasional

149

breaks in the vastness of the scene before us but otherwise the sand reached as far as the eye could see. The desert is beautiful in both its enormity and its solitude. One can only imagine the lives of those who work and thrive in such a setting. The camels marched almost silently over the soft sand surface as we went deeper and deeper into the heart of the Sahel, the section of the Sahara where we were traveling. Eventually, it was time to dismount and carry ourselves further on foot. Just reverse the process of starting out on a camel as described above and you know what it is like to get off and back on your feet. We began to walk toward the only visible structure on the horizon, a deep well containing a store of life-preserving water. We looked back at the two animals which had carried us during our beautiful ride. They stared at us in turn as if wondering who these creatures were that had disturbed their potential afternoon repose.

After examining the well as we passed by it, we soon came upon a few tents housing Tuareg families who lived their nomadic lives for the most part at that site. The structures were perhaps seventy to a hundred yards apart from one another and were built right on top of the sand with seemingly flimsy poles supporting a canvas-like covering and small mats standing in for flooring. That is how those families lived. The people smiled at us as we trekked past their solitary quarters. I suspect real estate is not very expensive in that corner of the world. Soon a major surprise appeared. A market sprang up before our very eyes. A number of the Tuareg men had gone back to their tents after they became aware of the presence in their midst of two Westerners and had brought out artifacts that they had either secured somewhere or created themselves. They formed a circle displaying these items in an organized way. Each of the men wore a carved knife with a scabbard hanging alongside his hip held on by a cloth belt. We carried no weapons with us at all and you can bet we bought a few artifacts there! The craftsmanship of the Tuaregs is exceptional; they produce excellent metalwork in a number of forms. So everyone left happy, we dragging along knives and other items we had purchased and they, counting the much needed money they had received from us. These basically itinerant Tuaregs are, for the most part, poor and unemployed these days. Living in the desert offers few work opportunities since the caravans no longer traverse the old trails north of Mali. A lovely knife with an amber handle and engraved blade I secured at that ephemeral market is one of my favorite artifacts. While I have several finely worked knives, none is more skillfully crafted than the one I bought in the desert.

A Little Misunderstanding

On another memorable occasion, at dinner in our modest hotel in the town of Divisadero in the heart of the Copper Canyon area in Mexico, we were the only two Americans in the place, but there was a group of several Spanish speaking guests seated at the next table. As we ate, I could not avoid overhearing the group talking among themselves about their plan to go on a horseback ride the following morning along the side of the canyon to look at its many picturesque views of the area. I related the conversation to Bev who had ridden a horse a few times before and who, I assumed, might have an interest in joining the ride. I strongly encouraged her to try it with the belief that it would be an interesting and memorable experience, which turned out to be very much as I had predicted. The fact that a woman much older than Bev was part of the group at the table, and who would presumably be riding with the group led us to believe that the ride would not be overtaxing. It never occurred to me to ask anyone if that older woman was going on the ride. I just inferred that she

151

was. We learned the next morning that she was not in the riding party, but it was too late then to take that into account. The entourage would only consist of three young, hearty Mexican couples and Bev along with the guide. As for myself, I had arranged a more comfortable and relaxed trek along the canyon side with a youngster from the area whom I met earlier on the train. It turned out that he lived in Divisadero and his mother worked in the very hotel where we were staying. He was to be my hiking guide.

First thing in the morning, the riders prepared for their excursion. Oh, what a mistake! Bev not only turned out to be 40 or so years older than the rest of the group but she was also the only one with little expertise in riding and, furthermore, the only one who spoke no Spanish at all. The others – the three couples and the leader of the group – spoke not a word of English. I remember standing by the departure point to make sure everything went along well. I noticed that the stirrups on Bev's saddle came down about ten inches too low for her to reach. No way was she going to get into them. Not a good start! I explained that to the guide, an old Mexican from the neighborhood without a sense of humor, who somehow got at least one of them up to the right height. The other never did make it to where it was supposed to be. Did I forget to mention that, Bev was not only deficient in Spanish and horsemanship, but she also was afraid of heights? I crossed my fingers as the group departed and I observed the look of fear and uncertainty on her face. Then I went on my hike.

I guess my first mistake was to ask Bev how the ride was when she returned. She harshly responded that it was one of the most horrifying experiences of her life. The horse she rode, it seemed, was also a bit lacking in English skills so it did not respond to a single instruction. Additionally, she could not complain or ask for help from the guide at all. Her horse meandered back and forth to the edge to view the valley from a dizzying height and each time she was convinced that she would go off the cliff. Finally, the guide noted her discomfort and wisely decided to tie her horse to his with a rope he had probably brought along for especially inadequate *gringos*. Wisely in part, that is. Another horse that was being ridden by one of the young Spanish speaking girls also had a distinct mind of its own. It just kept wandering off. The guide, with Bev's horse tied to his, had to keep going up the hill to the cliff side to steer the other girl's horse back onto the designated path. Instead of having her private occasional rides to the cliff's edge, it turned out that Bev's adventurous steed was now also going back and forth on the hill in order to keep another horse in check. After Bev almost collapsed from fright during the experience, she and the others returned to where they started. She was greeted by my friendly smile and my inquiry about her experience. It was just another recurrence of her occasional homicidal thoughts during our travels. I am not sure if she has gotten on a horse ever since.

A Lombok Treat

Lombok is an island in the Lower Sunda chain just east of Bali and part of the province of Nusa Tenggara, Indonesia. There are far fewer tourists there than on Bali but the island has some very lovely, sandy beaches as well as interesting cultural sites so it is worth several days for the tourist who has the time to spend. Fortunately, we were able to spend a few days there. One particular opportunity stands out in my mind as an intense experience in exploration. At breakfast in the hotel we stayed in on a beach in the town of Sengiggi in the north of the island, I was chatting with our waiter, Zohri. I inquired about the possibility of visiting a funeral or wedding ceremony on the island that was typical of the Sasak culture, the majority tribal group that lived there. He indicated that he had heard there was to be a funeral near his own village in the south and he could request the following day off and take me there. He also mentioned that he would love to visit his home on the trip and introduce me to his family. The whole undertaking sounded promising so I agreed to go. Zohri would be the bi-lingual guide and I would be the driver. I had already rented a car for the time we were staying on the island so I was all set. Bev declined to go with me. She felt worn out from our rather intensive travel, the drive would be long and so she chose to relax by the beach while Zohri and I toured for the day. Taking a day off from hard travel is something one should consider on any long trip. (I am not always good at taking my own advice in this respect.)

It turned out to be an amazing day. We stopped in small villages to walk around and see the people in action. I learned a great deal about the unique weavings the village people created and sold to tourists. There were two distinct styles of cloth-making called ikat[18] and songket[19] respectively which are so skillfully woven that high quality creations are

---

18   Ikat Cloth is a form of weaving in which the thread is dyed before it is woven by binding fibers around groups of threads to protect them from taking up color when the cloth is dipped into the dye. That is how the pattern is formed. Each island or region has its characteristic patterns, which serve to identify the area in which the cloth is made. In Lombok, Sumba and a few other places, the process is applied to the worp. Other forms of this weaving are weft ikat and double ikat. These weavings are difficult to make and are valued by collectors. In some places they also have ceremonial significance.

19   Songket is a hand-woven fabric decorated with metallic yarn on the surface of the fabric and is made throughout southern Asia in places like Malaysia and India as well as on some of the islands in the Sunda chain. It is also known as the cloth of gold thread although silver is often used and it is usually worn on special occasions. It is now made using artificial gold or silver threads in some places.

often sought by collectors. I saw this handiwork woven, dyed, dried and displayed. Their complicated processing and intricate design were the source of the value they often held for perceptive buyers. The local artisans also made a high quality of pottery and basketry.

Eventually, we reached the southern end of the island where the small village Zohri came from was located. We discovered that the funeral was not being held that day so that expectation was unfulfilled and I felt disappointed. But the time we spent at his home more than made up for the loss of witnessing a ceremony. When our car pulled up to the simple rattan walled, two room dwelling where Zohri's family lived and went into the house, we were quickly spotted and all the children in the village rushed over as we entered captivated by a Westerner coming into their area and entering one of the dwellings. Of course, they also knew Zohri and were equally curious about our association. As we sat on the floor in the hut, the kids peered at us from the open space above the low wall straining to peek over and see what was going on inside. Privacy was apparently not one of the underpinnings of that culture. And just what was going on there for them to observe? First of all, my guide was getting a tongue lashing from his mother about not visiting home for several months or even communicating with his parents. The young man was a bit embarrassed, but he was later welcomed quite warmly and enthusiastically by the entire family, especially a youngster of about 11 years old who was clearly excited to have his big brother home again after an absence of several months. We sat cross legged on the matted floor for about an hour sipping tea served by Zohri's mother while the family was enjoying the reunion. Zohri informed me while we were there about the gist of the discussion and I was intrigued by the interactions that unfolded before me. It was a truly intimate experience, and I was grateful for the opportunity to be a part of the group.

After we finally left the waiter's home, we roamed around the area a bit stopping briefly on the southernmost coast of the island where I discovered a totally isolated beach with a small bay that was as beautiful a seaside spot as I had ever seen. Zohri told me that a hotel chain was hoping to create a resort there. I never did find out if that happened but it would surely have been a great choice for the hotel although the roads leading down were a bit rough and the local culture would be strongly altered by the presence of such a resort. I asked Zohri why he had not visited home for a couple of months as it had taken us only a bit over two hours of driving to reach his village and there seemed to be so much joy at his arrival. The explanation was simple; taking buses with several connections from place to place required a full day of travel. Thus he needed at least three days for the trip, a major commitment. Our exchange of services was mutually beneficial as he had introduced me to aspects of his culture I would never have experienced and I saved him two days and quite a few Indonesian rupiahs. All in all, it was a very good barter indeed.

The Rice Farmer

In the neighboring island of Bali on another visit to Indonesia, Bev and I were strolling through rice fields to pass an afternoon. They were quite beautiful to look upon and the colors kept changing depending on how recently the rice had been planted. We came to one plot where the farmer was planting the young rice shoots he had grown from seeds earlier on. After the shoots reach a certain size and the field has been furrowed, they are placed in meticulous rows in the muddy ground. Farmers are quite careful about this to insure that the optimum distance between shoots is arranged and the maximum number of plants are fitted into the allotted space. Bev looked at the farmer and said she wished she could plant some rice. I encouraged her to inquire if she could do so at that very field. She communicated to the farmer that she wished to help with the planting, and he acceded to her request quite amiably. However, her planting apparently left something to be desired. After three or four shoots, the man indicated to her that the experience was over. She thanked him and we moved along. At least she was able to get her legs quite muddy and contribute, albeit negatively, to the rice production of that field. We both became more aware of how hard the work of those farmers is. Participating in what is transpiring in a setting is oft-times the only way to have the fun we relish on our trips.

Tourist Stops

Of course there are the usual traveler sites all over the world that offer assured satisfaction to the visitor in the form of famous buildings and geographical formations and historical locations, things that most voyagers underline in their guide books and prioritize before they leave home. These provide a special fulfillment and pleasure much like the sight of a rare bird offers to a dedicated birder. Can one go to India without a visit to the marble wonder that is the Taj Mahal, the legendary tomb of the wife of Shah Jahan? Would anyone willingly skip Angkor Wat or the other great nearby temples in Cambodia on a visit to that country? Could anyone resist the massive Buddhist structure of Borobudur north of Jogjakarta, Indonesia when access is within reach? That would be like skipping Notre Dame or the Louvre in Paris. These are buildings that one beholds and knows he has just reached one of the more important destinations a traveler can come upon. Add to these such sites as the Great Wall and the Imperial Palace in Beijing, the River Li as it meanders along the limestone cliffs that have been painted mistily and mysteriously by so many generations of Chinese artists and the other-worldly, terracotta Han army of countless soldiers and horsemen unearthed in Xi'an, one of the four ancient capitals of China.

Although the coast castles of West Africa stand tall among important visitation sites, in their case, it is not the architecture but their significance in the slave trade and the horrors which occurred in and around them that cause them to command our attention and pierce our souls. They, along with the concentration camps turned museums of Europe, the Killing Fields of Cambodia, the townships where Apartheid resistance was initiated in South Africa, all remain as memorials to horrors of the past centuries. And they are equaled in visitor appeal by the great colonial structures and pre-Columbian buildings that stand south of our own border where ancient cultures thrived. There are the Mexican pyramids from the giant structure called the Pyramid of the Sun at Teotihuacan outside of Mexico City to Mayan remains like the Castillo at Chichen Itza and the Pyramid of the Musicians at Uxmal, so perfect in form and so advanced in their astronomical perfection and structure. Further south, there stand other wonders of the Mayan period in jungle covered Tikal, Guatemala and Copan, Honduras, and the wonderful site of Palenque in the Mexican rainforest. On the other side of the equator stand the fascinating edifices of the Inca civilization of South America. And those are "just" buildings.

Could there be a more exhilarating sight than Victoria Falls with its spray reaching into the heavens and visible for miles around or the colors of the sky in the vast plains of Africa or the cloudlike, snow covered mountains of the Himalayas? The huge rice terraces of Bali and the Philippines are among countless other creations which often inspire awe in the observer. And many of the outposts of world history await the visitor from Biblical and other early religious sites like Mount Sinai or Mount Arafat, Mecca, Dharamsala, or remains of early cave painting or rock art, or great monuments to gods long gone along the Nile or paintings and statues of the Buddha in caves and carvings created along now abandoned trade routes through Asia. There are wonderful churches and mosques and temples which fascinate and enrich the Third World traveler as well. And one can access abundant art in various buildings from the monumental temples of Southern Asia and Mexico to those of Peru and Central America. In markets and museums one can see the incredible contemporary and recent workmanship of West Africa in textiles and bronze and wood which have inspired much of our modern design and imagination. In collections throughout the Third World, there are delicate ceramics and jewelry and other crafts from Japan and India and China, etc. Although I would not classify viewing art as simply fun, it can be enormously satisfying and memorable. This too is part of Third World adventure.

Coincidence in the Strangest Places

Among the most unexplainable events we have experienced in our journeys were times we encountered people whose presence along our travel route was exceptionally surprising. The first such occasion that I recall took place in the city of Puebla in Mexico many years ago. Puebla features a seemingly endless, authentic market of Indian vendors in a great open space so vast and crowded that one can easily lose track of their fellow travelers. It is truly a local market that features few tourist items but just about every kind of food and practical article for the homes and daily needs of the shoppers. In other words, it is not on the tourist route at all. I do not remember passing a single American as we threaded our way through the throng there. We were on a trip with our daughter, Jodi, who was a high school student at the time. Out of the midst of the crowd, we heard a call, "Yo, Jodi." At first we all thought our ears were deceiving us but that was not the case. From some assemblage of local shoppers emerged a fellow student in our daughter's class at school in Philadelphia. She, too, was visiting the market with her family. Incredible! Her visiting such an unlikely place at the very same time as we did was truly the essence of coincidence.

Another recollection I have of meeting someone in the most unlikely of places was in Bangkok. We stopped in a small, touristy store along a shopping street in the city and were looking around at the artifacts to secure a souvenir or two when a group of women from the States entered. We had seen virtually no Americans on our trip until then so we struck up a conversation with a couple of them. They asked us where we lived and we replied that we were from Philadelphia. One of the women indicated that she used to live in the city though she had moved to Florida many years ago and inquired as to what neighborhood we resided in. When we told her, she responded that we lived close to where she formerly lived with her husband who had died not long after they moved out of the city. She told Bev her name and Bev realized that the woman's husband was the very person she rode to school with when she was teaching some 15 years earlier until the couple left the area. We wound up meeting in Thailand to get the story of what transpired during those 15 years.

But similar things happen on a less dramatic scale with some regularity. Back in 1968 in Budapest, there were virtually no Westerners to be found as we traveled in the then Soviet controlled country. The beautiful capitol on the Danube was hardly a prime tourist destination at that time, at least not for Americans. We settled ourselves into a hotel with all the charm of the pre-war accommodations available in the great cities of Europe but without many of the contemporary amenities one might wish for. Our surprise occurred on the antique elevator connecting the several floors of the old building. Bev and I were speaking English, of course, when the only other person on the elevator began to speak to us. Her accent was clearly American. In our conversation we learned that, not only had we encountered another person from the States, but she came from our state and our city. It turned out that she lived about three blocks from our previous home in West Philadelphia. We encountered this one American in all of our Eastern Europe travel, and she lived a stone's throw away in our previous neighborhood. It was quite amazing.

Although this is a very different category of serendipity, the funniest encounter I ever had with someone I had previously met was at the border crossing between Kenya and Tanzania. On our way into the latter country from Nairobi, we stopped to present our documents at the immigration office. Right before we entered, we were assailed by a multitude of vendors selling the attractive wooden artifacts of the area. We decided we liked a particular necklace which featured several of the local animals, each carved and assembled skillfully into an interesting and attractive object. We engaged in lively bargaining as is the local custom in the area and bought a couple of the necklaces for $3.00 each. The seller did not seem totally happy with the transaction but we interpreted that as a salesman's posture to convince us that we did well and to encourage us to buy even more. The aftermath of this event ensued about 10 days or so later when we retraced our steps to reenter Kenya and continue our touring. We saw our Maasai vendor once more. I wanted to get another necklace or two for gifts and approached him to ask if he would like to sell us a few. He instantly responded to my inquiry with the comment, "Yes, but you aren't getting any for $3.00 apiece again." He had remembered the transaction as vividly as we had and we shared a wonderful laugh together. I imagine we had gotten his best price earlier. It was a busy sales station for this wily vendor and it was a wonder he recognized me.

Sometimes it seems the hand of fate turns the unlikely into a routine happening. One winter I had signed up to lecture on a cruise line on a trip to Southeast Asia. The ship on which I was supposed to work was attacked by pirates off the coast of Somalia on its cruise just before the stretch we were scheduled to go on. They cancelled my employment and explained that they needed our room for additional security guards they had taken on, although they generously agreed to pay our fare to the area so we could complete the plans we had made for travel after the cruise. I never imagined we would ascertain either what happened during the pirate attack or what the cruise was like that we were removed from. That is not until we walked along a street in Phnom Penh window shopping. We entered a store which featured local crafts and were looking around when another tourist entered. She was also from the States, she said. How had she reached Cambodia? She had been sailing on the very ship I was supposed to lecture on. She told us all about the arrangements we missed. It turned out that the cruise company had replaced the entire crew with new workers and had decided they did not want anybody who was involved in the pirate incident to be on the subsequent cruise. She also voiced her displeasure at the fact that none of the crew seemed to know what they were doing and thus the service and overall experience were disappointing for her. Since the ship was not at all the most significant part of our prior arrangement but rather merely a means to get to Southeast Asia again at little cost, we were quite satisfied with how things turned out. One more marvelous moment on the road.

More Surprises

It is almost always chance that brings us the most joyful happening in our travels. The unexpected, special and rare happenings that make one run to grab the camera, or stand transfixed at a window or in the middle of a street, or to suddenly be in the presence of a person unlike any other one has ever seen. A good example of this kind of recurrent experience was a time I stopped at a small restaurant along the road in Burma that leads from Mandalay to Lake Inle. The sound of music floated into the windows of our restaurant. I grabbed my camera and quickly went outside to witness a parade coming down the street. We asked our guide what the people were doing and got a most interesting explanation. This was a special celebration marking a young boy's entrance into residence at a nearby Buddhist monastery. It was the major initiation rite of his life and the beginning of his education among the monks. The child was dressed like a prince with finely woven, royal style clothing made for the occasion while his parents were adorned as the king and queen of the procession. They beamed with pride as they sat upon an ox-driven cart (even the animals were decorated for the occasion) trailing dozens of marching fellow citizens of their town who were also quite elaborately attired and carried a variety of foods, flowers and fancy items as offerings to the monks they would soon encounter at the monastery. It was an elegant and strange scene. I later learned that it was not the usual time of year for that particular event although it was a customary, rather common celebration in those parts after harvest time. But we had stumbled upon it nonetheless. My photos were some of the more arresting, attractive images of our entire trip.

Later, the same day along the very same road, we passed a quarter mile long row of people patiently waiting in line for some mysterious reason. I asked the driver to stop and I walked over to the beginning of the quiet column to find out why so many people were spending their time in line. I discovered that the government (the repressive, military establishment of the Myanmar Junta) was giving out candles free to the people who lived there. How generous! Candles! Not electricity or plumbing or some other commodity representing progress or civilization - candles! What could be a more illustrative measure of the status of the society than that line in the countryside? Ah, serendipity.

Of course, surprises and discoveries are not everyone's cup of tea. Emperors and kings were often carefully protected from unexpected happenings historically for their peace of mind and some tourists trade off possible spontaneity for the security of being taken care of - roughly the same kind of protection from stress. Had we been in a bus with a couple dozen other folks, we quite likely would not have been able to stop along the road at all. No happenings, no photos, no stories about the exceptional things we saw. For me, however, it was a day to cherish.

In some instances, taking chances in strange places has a component of danger as well. I might not be writing this book had I not allowed Bev to overrule me on one potentially foolhardy decision. In 1998 we were in Peshawar, the center of Muslim radicalism in Pakistan. I observed on my map that we were quite close to the Khyber Pass leading into Afghanistan. The Pass was a famous site in the history of the area and one of those exotic sounding places like Timbuktu that an adventurous traveler has floating around somewhere in the recesses of his brain. At the time, it did not seem like an overly foolhardy suggestion when I asked our guide to arrange to take us there before we headed up the Karakorum Highway toward China. He explained that we had to get government permission to drive that road and the authorization would include the provision of an accompanying car carrying several Pakistani soldiers to protect us. Apparently, there were terrorists or bandits even at that time right near the pass and they had been occasionally shooting at tourists in addition to committing other infringements of law and order. I said, "Let's go," and we drove to the office where permits were issued. As we walked toward the entrance, I heard Bev say something about being nervous, to which the guide replied, "So am I." Her response was that, if he was nervous, he did not need to worry one bit. We just were not going there. In spite of my initial disappointment, that was good enough for me. We turned around, I breathed a deep sigh at losing an opportunity to visit such a well known site, and we headed directly north toward the mountains we were to pass through for the next several days. This all took place before 9/11 so the extent of the danger was not something I had anticipated. In retrospect, score one for Bev.

Splurges

For the most part, especially the first 10 to 15 years of our Third World travel, Bev and I stayed in mostly simple places. On my very earliest trips, my stops tended to be in boarding houses, small *pensiones*, very modest hotels, etc. We eventually stepped up to higher class dwellings, if we could find them, mixed in with an occasional dump or two or a campsite here and there. In places like the tribal areas of India or the mountains of Pakistan or the small towns in Togo or Laos, the choices were quite simple regardless of one's preferences. Our concerns through that period were finances and a still present desire not to remove ourselves too far from the way the residents of the places we were visiting lived. We never deliberately selected the most primitive place in a particular destination but there were times when very basic settings were the only places available to tourists. I do want to mention three special accommodations that spring to my mind. These were so unique and enjoyable that they stand out as fun experiences on their own.

On our first trip to India, we landed in Delhi pretty much in the middle of the night. That was in the mid-1980s on our first long venture into Asia. I had made a reservation at the Taj Mahal Hotel in the newer section of the city after perusing my various guide books and doing some research. We were hardly prepared for what we saw. We entered the hotel when it was enveloped by the silence of an early morning hour and saw only one person at the reception desk and two or three workers mopping a beautiful, shining floor which was completely fashioned from multi-colored marble. The emptiness of the foyer enhanced our feelings of appreciation for the palatial building before us. The elegant setting welcomed us serenely and gently to what would be a three month voyage of hard traveling and stays at many far simpler dwellings throughout Southern Asia. Whatever that interminable plane ride wrought on our bodies seemed already to be worth the trip. The cost of the Taj at that time – about $60.00 a night – was remarkably low considering it was our big hotel splurge for the trip. In that instance, we were not at all living like most of the people we encountered afterwards. We were spending considerably more than we had to, but from our very first look around, we knew we would not match this place for the next months and we did not. No regrets about choosing to stay at the Taj. We have returned to India several times and on two of those occasions nostalgically wound up back at the same hotel. It is not considered the best nor most luxurious hotel in the city at this point in time, but it will always be our favorite. We had never seen anything like it in all of our previous travels. For Bev, who was a bit nervous about traveling through India, it was a great way to dispel her anxiety.

Another memorable experience took place quite a few years later when we stayed in a villa right on the beach in one of the San Blas Islands off the coast of Panama. We first flew by small plane from Panama City to the San Blas area. After arrival at the tiny landing strip on the largest of the islands, we were greeted by a local guide who doubled as our boatman during the days we spent there. We had arrived in the watery province of the colorful Kuna Indian tribe. Since it was late afternoon, we went directly to the tiny, palm-covered, totally private islet where we were to spend the next couple of days. On that sandy piece of Caribbean real estate there were just four cabins which extended into the calm, transparent water that lapped the beach. The only other building on the island was a small dining area with a separate attachment to house the Indians who attended us. The rest of the place consisted of just smooth, inviting sand and a couple of palm trees. Our cabin was more like a glorified permanent tent but it had a small shower and running water. It was a location that made us feel like jetsetters nestling into the privacy of some remote hideaway. Meals were provided by Kuna Indians who inhabit several of the approximately 400 islands that cover their semi-autonomous territory. The Kunas who attended to our needs caught and cooked a variety of fresh fish daily some of which probably swam past us as we toured in our boat the previous day. We considered the couple of days in that setting about as close to heaven on earth as anything we had ever done. As I mentioned, we are not beach dwellers, but sitting on the small porch of our building, we could see tropical fish flapping about, claiming and relinquishing territory as their neighbors wiggled around them; we watched water lapping slowly and methodically at the shoreline, and we especially enjoyed the show the sunset produced as evening approached. The beach was ours too. We dipped into the warm water at will, napped at the height of the day and rode in our boat to the surrounding islands for as long or as little as we wished. Our island may have been only a hundred or so yards around, but we felt we had all the space in the world at our disposal.

The final place I want to cite here was expensive, perhaps the most costly of any we have stayed in. We tend not to put very much money into our travel housing because we think of such places as mere resting sites for an evening in between days of adventure and challenge and learning. It is not our hotel rooms that we typically value. The River Club in Zambia was the most dramatic exception to that rule. On our first trip to the area, we designed our safari itinerary in southern Africa with the assistance of an agent who strongly recommended we stay at the River Club after we made clear we did not want to travel to Zimbabwe on our Victoria Falls visit. (No money for Mugabe). I no longer remember what the price of the room was although the trip itself was our most expensive as well. I do know the River Club was probably the most luxurious setting we have ever been in. The buildings consisted of a line of villas in a gardened area perhaps 50 yards from the shores of the Zambezi River a couple of miles before it empties into the falls. As we entered our cabin, we had a remarkable surprise: there was no back wall. It was a three walled building that consisted of an elegant bedroom on the walk-in ground level floor and a toilet and shower area below, both of which were totally open to the outside. One looked out onto the nearby shore of the Zambezi in which, even from our distance, we could watch hippos and crocodiles in the waters, fishermen in small boats earning their day's keep and rich, tropical vegetation all around. As evening descended, the picture changed and the river became softer. Hippos sought the dry shore, birds cried out for mates, and quiet and soft light made it all magical. Our bed was covered by a hanging mosquito net to protect us through the night. We needed no fan or air conditioner. The weather was as perfect as possible. I can still picture Bev, covered in bubble bath, resting in the bathroom tub looking out disbelievingly on the sights we shared from the back of our cabin. The stay may have been expensive but it was also totally unforgettable.

Even More Fun

Of course, fun has also included meeting interesting people, laughing together and exchanging adventures and life stories as well as passing on information about where to travel and what to do when you get there. Fun has included savoring the foods and wines which we would never have tasted otherwise. Fun was surprises like the currency drop one year we were traveling in Mexico which came about suddenly. We rushed to stores featuring American imports before the prices changed and picked up incredible bargains including some very cheap well-made American dress shoes. We also bought a few Aztec statues we could not have normally afforded which now stand on our fireplace mantel. The shoes are long gone but the statues remind us every day of our alert bargain hunting. Or our first South African trip which was greatly enhanced when the rand fell by over 50% and we went from modest living to having tasty local wines brought to our table for $5.00 per bottle, and we hardly looked at the right side of the menu when selecting luxurious and delicious dishes. Fun was also doing silly, touristy things like dressing up in local costumes in southern China to take pictures of ourselves or dancing the tango for the first time in Argentina. Fun included trips into mines in Bolivia and Brazil, scuba diving without certification in the South Pacific, getting tipsy on vodka in Cold War Russia or on the local liquors on Monkey Island Road in Bali. Fun was bargaining for native products and realizing that there was only a nickel difference between our offer and the asking price while we seriously pondered the wisdom of completing the purchase (one can get lost in such negotiations). I would contend that that many of the challenges were also fun. Our research into how long one could travel without the clothing we originally brought along was amusing. Our luggage was standing alone in some corner of an African or Asian airport. Sitting in an open vehicle a few yards from a yawning lion which appeared as uninterested in us as was imaginable was fun. Walking along the misty path across from Victoria Falls and getting totally soaked by the spray was pure fun. Fun was also walking through Ho Chi Minh's Mausoleum and, in the midst of the reverence and silence that pervaded the building, imagining he would soon get up out of his glass coffin and greet us. More fun was a train ride from Calcutta to Darjeeling sharing a cabin with the head of the police of the latter area and a Muslim who wanted to know everything about Judaism and would have stayed up the entire night to talk with us had we possessed the energy. Offering to buy a loaf of the delicious country bread in a small village in Turkey as it was being carried on a tray on a woman's head and being first gifted with a loaf and then led to the kiln where it was baked was fun. Ordering blindly by pointing to one of the pots on the stove in an isolated Greek restaurant where no one else spoke English was fun even if we wound up picking meat off a bone which turned out to be a goat's head before we were aware of what was in our plate. Bev just happened to notice my meal staring at her. We were a bit hungry later but we did have a great laugh. Tasting tropical fruits we had never seen before was a special treat in almost every equatorial area we traversed. Stopping to interact with kids at village schools or talking with a group of youngsters who are studying English and answering their questions about America is fun. Riding a camel through the gorgeous rock formations in the Sinai Desert or into the endless Sahara sands or renting one just to sit on so we could better observe the festivities at a fair in India was fun. Of course, getting home and actually seeing the results of my photography has always been one of the most enjoyable parts of every trip we have taken.

The more we interact with the people we visit, the more fun we have. In West Africa there were endless opportunities to bond with people in the many hospitable tribal villages. One of the best examples of this that I recall was a time we were the only overseas visitors watching a stilt dance performance at a village get together. We learned it was the custom for people to place a few coins on the ground and challenge the dancers to pick them up while bending forward on their stilts. At a certain point, I walked out to the middle of the dance area and put down a few West African francs. The dancers successfully manipulated themselves into position, picked up the money and bowed to us. Everyone cheered and we felt as much a part of the crowd as anyone else in attendance. A similar thing happened at a funeral in Indonesia after we were invited to join a dance line. A can was being passed for a collection to help defray the considerable expenses of the ceremony and the people truly appreciated our contribution and our participation. We have also gotten up to dance with the local people in many villages in West Africa and in rural India after we were invited to do so. Similar opportunities presented themselves in Kenya and Swaziland and many other places. These seem like small things but they do make a difference to the folks we visit and they are good memories for us as well. Just getting up to join the celebration actively in a small African or Asian village at some local festival or event is an act of unity and respect and is inevitably well received. There are times when one becomes involved in events which can seem quite strange when viewed analytically but which are quite natural to the people you are visiting. On at least two occasions, for example, we were asked to give our autograph to groups of people in Borneo and in Sulawesi. That is something I would have thought silly had it occurred at home or some more familiar place, but it was clear that our presence was special for the groups of young people who solicited our signatures so we went along with the process and had the experience of being celebrities at least those two times in our lives. Sometimes I have felt quite foolish doing such stuff but I have never once regretted it. Visitors tend to be judged, not by their skills or their appearance but by the spirit and attitude they bring along with them. The ugly American is not one who disappoints by making an effort to fit in and falters but one who disdains getting up to try.

Actually, almost all the things I have done on my travels can be classified as fun to some extent with the possible exception of the relatively few times I was conscious of some tension between me and the local residents or faced potential injury or danger to me or Bev. One can only relish those types of occasions in retrospect. Such instances have been rare and they have never slowed down my ongoing joy of the road.

Young boatmen navigating the Mekong River near Luang Prabang, Laos

Woman smoking a cheroot, a type of local cigar, in the countryside, Vietnam

Tarascan Indian woman in Michoacan, Mexico

Flute Player in the Udayagiri Caves near Bhubaneswar, India

CHAPTER SEVEN

POLITICS AND TRAVEL

"Perhaps travel cannot prevent bigotry, but by demonstrating that all peoples cry, laugh, eat, worry, and die, it can introduce the idea that if we try and understand each other, we may even become friends."

— Maya Angelou

As I look around the world with its seemingly limitless opportunities for fruitful travel, one consideration I always take into account in selecting my next destination is the political situation that exists in the country, not only in respect to how the journey might affect us but also how our travel might impact the people we interact with there. There are basically two points of view about going to places dominated by illegitimate rulers who oppress the people. In some places, foreign travelers are encouraged to visit although they are sometimes prohibited from doing so by the government of their intended destination which prefers to keep the status of its citizens as little known as possible. Many years ago I was refused a visa to visit Stalinist Russia. A strong current example that comes to mind is North Korea. The idea behind encouraging the visiting of undemocratic places is that contact with outsiders is beneficial for the people, that residents can get more information from tourists about happenings in their own country, and that the money brought in by travelers, if distributed directly to the public and not to government owned institutions, can benefit the poorest and neediest of citizens. Of course, the opposing argument is that you cannot keep all the money you spend out of the government's hands because they usually own the modes of transportation and other important tourist services (see: Burma, China, Zimbabwe.) Secondly, visitors help to legitimize the government and keep the world from isolating autocratic nations. I tend to usually favor the second argument so we have chosen to pass up otherwise tempting destinations on many occasions, but I appreciate both points of view and I always try to think a situation through before deciding about the political implications of our travel choices.

Burma (Myanmar now) was clearly the most difficult recent choice we made. After much consideration we decided to go there. Among the people and organizations whose stance about that choice I was aware of, opinion was about equally divided although the imprisoned Nobel Laureate, Aang San Suu Kyi, personally discourages visitors. Other Burmese expatriates and opposition leaders have indicated that tourists are welcome or even needed. Bev and I had been there some 20 years before our most recent trip under different circumstances so I factored in my age, added my burning desire to see the changes that had transpired over the intervening time and augmented that with my eagerness to explore more fully this fascinating nation and decided to go. One can never really calculate the net results of such a choice but the people I interacted with seemed quite pleased that we had come. What we tried to do to whatever extent possible was ensure that the bulk of our dollars for expenditures went straight into the hands of the people who served us. We also took in a few magazines and books to leave there for information starved people who desired them. While the ruling Junta has since made clear that they have an iron, uncaring grip on that unfortunate land by their behavior in relations to elections, the uprising of the monks and their abominable response in the aftermath of the floods of 2008, our journey took place before those happenings. Their more recent dealing with Aang San Suu Kyi has been even worse. I felt our contributions to temples along the way, tips to boatmen or porters, purchases of artifacts from vendors and taxi rides from place to place still brought a measure of happiness and appreciation to the faces of the needy people we encountered. We were keenly aware of the repressive environment in Burma while we were there and what our political footprint might be as we interacted with Burmese along the way. One of our constant acts was to let people know that the outside world was quite knowledgeable in respect to the actions of the government and the political repression the people there faced and we let them know how sympathetic we were personally to the plight of the citizens of the country. We also informed people about the organized citizen support for them that existed in the United States. I think that was a comforting revelation for some folks with whom we spoke. We also made sure to respect the hesitation and fears of those who were reluctant to discuss their personal plight under the generals[20]. There was no difficulty distinguishing those who were opposed to the government among the folks we met; they all were.

20   The generals referred to here are the members of the ruling Junta. Than Shwe has been the top figure in the junta since 1992, when he replaced Saw Maung, the leader of a military coup four years earlier. There are a total of eleven generals who rule the country. They are the ones who refused aid during the terrible cyclone of 2008 and shot or imprisoned many monks who demonstrated earlier in Myanmar. The current government still holds the rightfully elected prime minister, Aang San Suu Kyi, under house arrest as I write these words.

We have had several such experiences like that one including a similar occasion I remember which occurred in The Soviet Union in 1971. At that time, there was an active movement on the part of many members of an oppressed Jewish population there to secure freedoms which were denied to them, especially the right to freely emigrate to more welcoming nations where they could practice their religion without shame and discrimination. At the time, Jewish presses were silenced in the country; there was no printing of prayer books nor was there production of religious items. Important jobs were unavailable to Jewish citizens as well and emigration was quite difficult. The treatment of Jews was surely not the only objection Westerners had to visiting the area during the height of the Cold War but it was a significant additional factor for quite a few. The international movement to free Soviet Jews had already begun to spread through the United States, Western Europe and Israel. Bev and I were traveling through Scandinavia with our young kids that summer and we decided to join an international group of travelers on a five day bus trip to Leningrad (now St. Petersburg) from Helsinki. Earlier I wrote about our vodka night in the hotel? That was the only humorous episode on that trip. One of the things we were clear about was that we wanted to distribute religious items to members of the Jewish community, not an easy task. Our opportunity came when we arranged to visit the Great Synagogue of Leningrad. Unfortunately, there were few worshippers present on the weekday afternoon we chose to visit the building. We were greeted right at the entrance by the Shamus, the layperson who is usually responsible for moment to moment matters in a synagogue including such issues as book distribution, preparations for services, and so on. He engaged us as we entered to explain at length how supportive the governing regime was to the Jewish community there. He claimed they supplied books and other artifacts necessary for worship. We knew better. Those lies were a transparent effort to mislead us. He was actually a government employee and his job depended on such deception. His actual purpose was to spy on the congregation and to make sure that tourists did not "misinterpret" what they were seeing.

I had smuggled in several small religious items including mezzuzahs[21] and Stars of David. We were determined to pass them on to those who could not otherwise access such artifacts but that was a little tricky. While Bev distracted the Shamus with simple questions, I was able to sidle up to a worshipper who was standing in a pew in prayer and slip him the objects we had smuggled in. He was so nervous, he was barely able to acknowledge the effort but I felt quite certain the items were much appreciated. I am not recommending that Third World travelers to autocratic nations imitate such behavior although it was rewarding to perform even such a small service in a land where people had so little freedom.

Being around political activities was nothing new for us. During the summer of 1968, we often found ourselves in the vicinity of many of the disruptions, protests, and clashes between police and revolutionaries that characterized the period. We were motoring through Europe with our young children at the end of my year teaching at the Overseas School of Rome. Every place we went seemed to be brimming with tension and turbulence. In St. Mark's Square in Venice, I recall seeing a developing confrontation between a police squadron and a group of youthful

---

21   A Mezzuzah is a small cylindrical container made of metal or wood or ceramic which contains a piece of parchment with writing on it from the Sh'ma, a Jewish prayer, *i.e.* the phrase, ("Hear O Israel! The Lord our God, the Lord is one!" Deuteronomy 6:4). The object is customarily mounted on the frame of the entrance door to a house or worn on a chain around a person's neck.

demonstrators. The scene promised violence and arrest. I did not want Bev to miss the action so I quickly ran back to our room not far from the square, took her with me and ran back to see what transpired That encounter turned out to be a bit much even for us. As the face-off materialized, shots were fired into the air. Bev and I hurriedly ducked under a metal overhead storefront cover which closed behind us and separated us from the events that were unfolding. When it was raised again, the square was clear except for a whiff or two of tear gas and the skirmish was over. We never did find out the results of that incident, but we inferred that the demonstrators wound up in the local jail at the very best. I am well aware of the fact that Venice is not at all a Third World location, but the kind of activity we witnessed during that time is not typically witnessed in the developed areas of the West these days. As a matter of fact, in 1968 the entire city of Venice was filled with revolutionary graffiti much of which was on display all over the bicentennial art celebration that was going on in the city.

Two stops we made after Venice brought home to us powerfully the politics of the East at the time, especially in Hungary and Czechoslovakia. In Budapest, we saw the hushed, artificial tranquility of oppression. Everything was quite in order. There was an abundance of Hungarian soldiers enforcing the Soviet-style, unrepresentative government that was then in power. It had been many years since 1954 when the people of Hungary first attempted to free themselves from the Soviet yoke and briefly rejoiced at a seeming success that soon unraveled in the face of military power.

Prague was another story altogether. We arrived shortly after a new government had been installed by the Czech people, heralding what came to be known as the Prague Spring; it was a westward looking government that claimed independence from the Soviet Union and it was almost universally popular with the citizens of the country. We were in the first country that had "successfully" separated itself from the Eastern bloc and the excitement was palpable. I could not count the number of people who came up to us to practice their language skills or who offered to exchange currency, delirious in their anticipation of a better future. They were going to travel west they thought, and quite soon. They would need Deutschemarks or dollars. We had none of the former and too few of the latter to be helpful. People conveyed their joy and their plans to us (in German for the most part because the area had suffered greatly not too long before from their northern neighbor). They had finally had enough of authoritarianism and were determined to stay free. They succeeded in doing so for but two more weeks. We were driving through France on our way to Paris when the news came over our radio that Soviet troops had entered Prague. The government was overthrown, a puppet leader was installed and the brief moments of freedom were over. Breaking free had been an illusion but the pain that followed was nonetheless quite substantial. We literally cried as we heard the details. The people we had met in Prague were very much in our mind throughout the remainder of our journey. It was to be many more years before the world changed for them.

Paris was also one of the centers of protest in Europe. One seemed not to be able to walk anywhere in the city without some reminder of how unique the summer of 1968 was. There were demonstrations one place or other every day we were there. It did not crimp our touring style too significantly because the museums and parks remained open but the tear gas that wafted into our window from picturesque squares not too far from the hotel where we resided kept us mindful of the unusual circumstances of our tour of Europe.

181

Where Shall We Travel Next?

Sometimes, it seems that everywhere we go there is some level of dissatisfaction with the local government on the part of a segment of the people, some problem that cannot be resolved in what most people would consider a reasonable and democratic way, some prevailing system of authority that inhibits individual liberty. I run across people marching, demanding, praying or begging for changes to make their lives better. I have been present at incipient riots in Chiapas, Mexico, witnessed angry peasants demanding fairer treatment in La Paz, Bolivia and Guayaquil, Ecuador, viewed Basque separatists in San Sebastian, Spain insisting that their comrades be released from jail, spoken with relatives of the Disappeared asking for justice in Argentina, been stalled at road blocks on the rural roads of tribal India where people were protesting government policies toward their region and on and on. Neither the industrialized world nor the Third World offers an inviolable guarantee of justice to every one of its citizens but the people of Africa, South America and much of Asia are often struggling actively to achieve an assurance of political freedom, fairness and justice. It seems that someone always has to put him or herself on the line to make the slightest progress in many of those areas. I am both mindful and respectful of that reality.

As a matter of fact, when I looked over the map from time to time to plan what direction to take for my next Third World expedition, I often had the feeling that there was no place to go that was totally free from personal conflict about whether or not a decision to travel to that location could be justified. For example, China, especially during my first trip in 1986, was the same repressive country that clamped down at Tiananmen Square three years later and jailed hundreds of innocent people some of whom remain incarcerated even today in order to enforce the government's control of its people. My second trip to that destination occurred while the government was suppressing the Muslim minorities in their West with whom they remain in active conflict even to this very day. Our travels to Indonesia occurred before the East Timor massacres yet we were quite aware of the record of that government's quashing of human rights and political freedom, especially through the formative years of the country under first Sukarno and then the army and Suharto. I have already mentioned Burma but Vietnam was also quite an autocratic government when we visited it as was neighboring Cambodia. In West Africa, although I moved amongst only those countries where there was no active internal insurrection at that time, the regimes where I visited were hardly democratic. Of course, I did rule out immediately places like Liberia and Sierra Leone where petty dictators were chopping off hands and feet from time to time. Even today, only twenty or so African nations possess any meaningful level of democracy. The rest are either outright dictatorships or one party states. In South and Central America the gap between the poorest and the richest citizens is exemplified by the desperate poverty one encounters in the villages or in the *favelas* and other slums in the cities which stand in stark contrast to the new, fancy condominiums built alongside beautiful beaches. To whom would our money go in those lands? Was the level of economic injustice we observed more insupportable than the political repression in other lands. And what does all that mean in respect to travel choices anyhow?

Even as I write these words, I ponder where I would or would not visit if I were planning a trip right now. After the government's handling of first the protests and then the cyclone, I know I would not go back to Burma. Even the possibility that the Junta might profit slightly from my presence would be enough to dissuade me now that they have gone so far as to prevent international aid from reaching their starving citizens. Nor could I bring myself to visit as punitive and terrorized a place as North Korea where the repression of the citizenry has reached such fantastic levels. Were the devils still in power in Sierra Leone or their counterparts in Liberia, safety considerations aside, I would refuse to visit there also. With the kind of religious repression represented by its Wahabist government, I would choose to avoid places like Saudi Arabia as well. We could go down the list from totally loathsome and morally reprehensible regimes to merely disagreeable and objectionable ones. Where is the tipping point? Choices are often difficult and may well be quite arguable as well. For us, no Sierra Leone visit while the government was cutting off the hands of their citizens and kidnapping children for their army. No South Africa while Apartheid was the law of the land. No North Korea while the people are systematically starved because of government policies. No Sudan while slavery reigns and villagers are raped and terrorized. No Rwanda during the time the populace was encouraged to slaughter one another. (I fear I shall never see the great gorillas in that land.) No Guatemala or Nicaragua while U.S. supported militias were quashing indigenous movements. The cutoff point is some level of horror that is so egregious, I would never want to be associated with it. And even that is perhaps more of an intestinal reaction than a logical one.

Traveling with Repression

Countries which suffer from political oppression significantly differ from one another in respect to how controlled the visitor's movements are. I remember from early in my travels what it felt like to take the train sponsored by the U.S. military that connected Frankfurt with West Berlin during the days that Germany was divided between the Cold War foes which had split up the nation. The train ran during the dark hours of the night and it reached East

Germany about 2:00am when it was almost impossible to discern much in the blackness outside except for a few occasional dim house lights in one village to another. The mysteries that lurked behind those faint illuminations were left to the imagination of the traveler. In any event, the curtains of the train were drawn rather fully and we would not have seen much even during the daytime. What we did know was that there would be stops at the border, passing of documents and passports to the guards from the East, and a quick departure into the strange land followed by our arrival in West Berlin a night's sleep later. The train itself was rather dark and most of the passengers slumbered throughout the trip. The East Germans successfully kept anyone on the train from having even minimal contact with the people we were passing or even from knowing the slightest about what any of the circumstances were like for those who lived in the towns and villages where those few lights shined. That, of course, was the perfect setting for repression- darkness, isolation, mystery.

Interestingly enough, for a good stretch of the period of Germany's partitiion, it was possible to take the elevated train in Berlin to go from West to East and back. Mini-visits to East Berlin revealed the lack of post-war reconstruction and the bleakness of the streets and stores and interiors of buildings that characterized much of the East at the time. One could speak with people but not extensively or openly. Caution ruled. The best a western traveler could do was exchange some West German marks for their eastern equivalents (at about four or so to one) and buy incredibly cheap goods. The choices were quite limited however. The people were quite happy to receive West German money though there was very little to buy. I did purchase some books (much of it Soviet propaganda but with good photography at times) and many records (back in the vinyl days.) The orchestras of the East from places like Moscow and Leningrad were quite good, especially at Russian symphonic music.

Many years later, I was able to visit Leningrad as I indicated earlier. Aside from the vodka and caviar experience in our hotel, most of my time in the city left negative memories. I had the most palpable feeling of repression and control that I ever experienced as a traveler anywhere. Our hotel had someone posted on every floor, someone who seemed to be assigned to watch the comings and goings of the guests, there were KGB looking characters on street corners, and people were quite reluctant to interact with foreigners insofar as I could tell. Of course I did not have the language skills that would have afforded me a more intensive and informative experience were such available. I did not find the people pleasant or forthcoming at all. I distinctly recall one very memorable moment. I was in one of large department stores (#1 or #2 or #3, I don't recall) and I took out my camera to take a photo of the unattractive, very limited items on sale in the clothing section. A saleswoman immediately came over and started shouting at me to put my camera away. I was not only embarrassed but I felt threatened and was worried for myself and the camera equipment I was using, so I quickly complied. I am always sensitive to photographing poverty or distress but what I was taking pictures of was more a result of political circumstances than anything else. I do not think it was shame that brought the saleswoman over to interrupt me but rather duty to her government. She was likely there for security purposes- security of accurate images I suppose. If so, that is an ugly thing. When one cannot photograph a showcase of clothing for sale, repression surely hangs heavy on the people.

There were to be many other times when I was surrounded by tyranny or government cruelty in my travels. I have spoken about Burma and the oppression of the people in that country. The visitor, however, does not bear the brunt of this phenomenon in the same way as I have described in Soviet Russia. People are sunnier, more willing to carefully discuss their circumstances, and goods are attractive and available to people who can afford them. Of course, propaganda is ubiquitous as is poverty and lack of technology. China in the 1980s was despotic but small businesses seemed to flourish and folks competed for the attention (and especially the money) that tourists could offer. Post-war Yugoslavia was a place one could engage people in conversation about politics and the future in spite of Tito's heavy hand. Vietnam in the 90s, even though the country was dominated by a controlling Communist government, enabled tourists to roam totally freely, constructed a variety of resources for the many visitors that had begun to flow into the country and was quite a pleasant place as a travel destination.

Repressive societies vary in their impact upon the subjects who live within the grasp of their despotic regimes, but they especially differ greatly in how they affect visitors. It is hard to laugh and even harder to relax in places where folks are not free to express themselves or to interact genuinely with their counterparts from other places in the world.

The Moral Implication of Third World Travel

I believe that all of our actions have a moral component. That notion very pointedly includes choices about where and how we travel. Now that ecotourism is an option, many more travelers have begun to take note of our carbon footprint and try to take that into account along with political considerations. Our political footprint is equally significant. One can travel, learn about a culture or nation and still make a positive statement at the same time. There has long been an issue for anthropologists who study traditional cultures in respect to how intrusive and impactful

187

their observations may be; that should also be a concern for those who frequently visit very remote places where many residents have little or no experience dealing with visitors from more technologically advanced areas. Seeing yourself for the first time in a Polaroid print some years back or currently in a digital image may not be earthshaking but it does leave a residue, a glimpse of a world which promises other possibilities, other prospective living circumstances that may be viewed as more desirable. This kind of interaction and additional potentially culture modifying contacts with curious guests can intrude upon the precise traditional aspects of a society that make it an object of interest in the first place and can interfere with or distort natural development that might normally take place in such a setting. As our world shrinks, cultures experience more and more strange intrusions from other places willy-nilly. The traveler should be wary of adding to that inexorable phenomenon.

Embarrassed Embara

An excellent example of what I would consider to be a destructive interchange between visitors and the residents of a traditional society was the contrast I observed during two separate visits I made to a group of indigenous people in Panama eight years apart. The ethnic inhabitants were the Embara Indian tribe who live in the jungle away from the westernized cities of Panama. Most of their recent history has been spent quite apart from the surrounding culture. The Panama Canal was built and eventually transferred to the government of that country while they still hunted and foraged for subsistence. Governments rose and fell around them with little impact on their way of life. In the year 1999, when my wife and I were first there, I don't recall seeing any other visitors on my trip into the forest where the Embara live. The Indians I met, especially the kids, were curious about us and seemed to be living quite simply in their jungle surroundings. The women were naked from the waist up. The prepubescent kids wore very thin cloths covering their genitalia; and the youngest among them wore nothing at all. The adults performed unpretentious and very authentic dances on our behalf in an open community gazebo after which we had a light lunch together. We brought some food of our own on the visit and shared what we had with them. I told my family about that visit eight years later when I hoped to replicate the good experience Bev and I had for the edification of our grandchildren. I also wanted to make sure the kids would be respectful of this very different culture. But the second time we appeared in the same village, the scene was significantly changed. This time, the women were more fully covered, the dancing and music more sophisticated and formal, and lunch was cooked and served to us by the Indians. The kids from the village were at school down river when we arrived. They returned home dressed far more modestly and formally than I had seen them on my last visit but they quickly rushed into their huts to change into more comfortable leisure clothing even though these second simple, less dressy outfits left them much more covered than eight years earlier. They had obviously been instructed to conceal most of their body when visitors were there. Initially they even seemed to want to hide the fact that they normally wore a distinctly un-Embara like uniform for school. So much of what we saw on that second visit was staged.

One reaches the forest of the Embara in canoes which were already motorized in 1999 and which seated four to six people each. On our first trip, I recalled feeling alone and quite at peace floating along on the winding, shallow jungle river. When our family group went later on, we perceived a fleet of nine or so boats coming or going. The jungle walk with our native guides which I recalled from our earlier visit had not changed much but the people's daily lives had been altered considerably. They no longer hunted because the government had ruled that they could not continue to do so. Instead, their income was based entirely on the tourist show they had turned into. We were informed that modifications in their dress had been made because earlier tourists from South America leered and laughed at the women and were generally offensive to the Embara people they were visiting. As for the hunting, it just had no place in a setting with so many guests nor was it any longer necessary because there was now a steady income from the tourist agencies which provided sufficiently for the group's daily needs. Life had indeed changed for the Embara and the main cause was the tourist footprint.

We all need to be aware of our part in that process. For those who care about the welfare of the peoples and places they visit as well as the kind of world we ultimately leave to our children, travel planning needs to be responsible and careful, and touring needs to be as harmless and gentle as we can make it. The fine print may now be in our footprint.

Whatever the politics of the countries we visit, we should feel obligated to demonstrate a decent measure of respect for the cultures we interact with. When I think about the effect the South American guests had on the Embara, I realize how detrimental tourism can be at its worst. If we go to places without bringing our sensitivity and kindness along, if we are not tolerant of the ways that others meet daily tasks and celebrate life events and how they arrange their respective priorities in line with their understanding of the world around them, we would be better off not mixing with other societies around the world and they would certainly be better off not having us in their midst. We need not share the values of people who cause pain to their animals, or treat their women or children in a disrespectful, punitive manner or are superstitious or guarded or aggressive in ways we would not choose to be, but we are the outsiders. We cannot be their judges. It is not for us to condemn the behavior of people whose lives are constructed quite differently from ours by virtue of their history or geography or beliefs. Are there issues we want to involve ourselves in? Of course, but that is not the role of a tourist, it is the function of an activist. Would I be pleased to have female circumcision ended in West Africa? You bet. And would I contribute to or offer my time and energy to a group dedicated to such an end? Absolutely. Do I object to governments that fail to provide their citizens the education or financial opportunities or worker's rights that should be part of every person's birthright? Not only do I object to such things but I try to participate helpfully in groups that work toward a better world for impoverished and undereducated people all over. But that is another function of my life and should not be confused with the tourist role I assume during my travels. My interactions with farmers in Mali is for my edification, not theirs. What I learn from such contacts informs my political thinking and activity and makes my travel an important aspect of my learning. When I go to tribal areas, the agent I select to help me make arrangements must demonstrate a commitment to the ongoing welfare of the group or groups I intend to visit. This can be achieved in several ways but contributions to the wellbeing of the indigenous people in the form of support of social services or medical facilities or literacy or economic development projects for the group or village are very clear behaviors a travel company can exhibit to show that it cares about more than the bottom line. That is the kind of agency I would recommend people to use for exotic voyages to tribal areas. In planning our itineraries for safaris in Botswana and in South Africa, I made sure that we stayed only at camps which had partnered with and employed people from neighboring villages. That is one way of benefitting the nearby villagers as well as paving the way for the guests at the safari camps to visit and interact comfortably with the residents of the cooperating villages.

Visiting Recent History

While taking a trip can offer great enjoyment, intense beauty, introduction to strange and interesting peoples and new foods and activities, it can also bring one close to important events and eras of the past, many of which we may well be already familiar with. In South Africa, for example, there is a ferry which takes one from Capetown to the prison on Robbens Island where Nelson Mandela was incarcerated for many years along with other important figures in the African National Congress and in the overall movement to end Apartheid. That trip is an especially moving experience. After a bus tour of the island itself which includes the prison area, the barracks, the lovely views back toward Capetown, and even the colony of African penguins that lives on the coastline of the island, tourists are deposited near the entrance to the prison which is now maintained as an educational center to inform locals and visitors alike of the cruelty of the former government and the repressive policies which it created and enforced as well as to teach folks about earlier uses of the site beginning with its original function as a leper colony. At the entrance each group is met by a guide who instructs the guests about life in the compound and takes them through each area to explain what life was like there for the prisoners. And he performs that task quite knowledgably. All the guides are former prisoners themselves. Each one spent much of his youth in the cells and halls and worksites of that institution. We saw Mandela's cell and the bed he slept in for seventeen years of his life. A moment of silence and respect came over our entire group. On my second trip to the island, the one I took with my family, the youngest of my grandsons who was only eight years old at the time considered that excursion the highlight of our journey even compared to the incredible animal sightings we had observed on our safari. I guess he was also impressed.

On an earlier experience In Vietnam, a detour from my planned route turned out to be another very special visit, one of my most valuable and meaningful on that journey. I had been surprised by the overall friendliness that people we met showed toward Americans since we came from a country that only a single generation earlier had been bombing their land and mining their ports. Why did they seem to welcome our presence more than tourists from most other countries who visited them? That question is still unanswered for me. At any rate, we took a detour to stop at My Lai, where the terrible massacre of 347 people, mostly women and children, all unarmed Vietnamese peasants, was perpetrated by American forces during the war. Some victims were sexually abused, others beaten or tortured or maimed or mutilated in that unfortunate and shameful incident. While I have visited several sites of massacres in our travels, this was the first one I viewed which was caused by our own forces and it was a powerful experience in many ways. First of all, the little village that once stood on those grounds has been turned into a museum. Bullet holes in trees, air raid shelters where grenades were thrown on folks trying to escape the attack, what was left of shacks used for cover have all been left in place. There is a small building at the site which houses maps and figures and photos of the events. Starkly depictive statues stand around outside on the grounds. Signs mark the spots where the murders and other atrocities were committed. Everywhere one looks, the horror of war and the inhumanity of man confront the viewer. Yet the people who live there and maintain the site are gentle, peaceful and friendly. They presented a marvelous contrast to the scene as well as an enigmatic one. I saw other visitors from the United States who were former soldiers who had come to the site for their personal reasons, penitence perhaps, maybe peacemaking - who knows what? We spoke with them, we interacted with the few survivors, we looked around at the harmless rice fields surrounding the village, we bowed our heads in reverence and respect, and we went on our way back to the itinerary that originally had neglected to include that indispensable visit.

I guess it was somewhat easier for us to visit the Killing Fields of Cambodia. At least America was not directly involved in the atrocities that transpired there. But the magnitude of the genocide of millions that occurred in that country thanks to the Pol Pot regime was nonetheless overwhelming. The Cambodian government has preserved and memorialized the places where the murders took place in an interesting but macabre way. There are towers which contain countless skulls piled on top of one another alongside piles of clothing stripped from the bodies they once covered; these are all open to the outside air and subject to the touch of visitors. Schools which were turned into prisons and torture chambers stand in silent testimony to the victims. And the fields themselves are littered with shards of bones shattered by gunshots or crushed underfoot when the riddled bodies of doomed Cambodian victims had sufficiently decayed. It is indeed a horrifying sight probably because one becomes intimate so quickly with the details of what transpired there. The fields are unburied cemeteries, memorials to the disregard shown by the Khmer Rouge for the Cambodian people who suffered and died so that complete political power could be attained by a government that will go down in shame forever in the annals of mankind.

But a visit to historical sites can also be a tribute to positive social change, a means to honor the conquests of mankind or the heroes who led the way to better times over the years. Memorials to Mahatma Gandhi in Delhi and Mumbai and other places mark the effect upon the entire world of this admirable figure who changed the landscape of the Indian nation and showed the rest of us another way to achieve progress between enemies. Statues which pay tribute to the ultimate end of West Africa's slave trade and the freeing of people from that horrendous cultural desecration line the coast in Benin and Ghana and Senegal. Mandela's cell in Robben's Island Prison is indeed a sad and dreary place but it was also the residence he left from to become one of Africa's great leaders. One can visit sites that mark important moments and events that remind us of the Buddha and Jesus and other great preachers of peace even though thousands of years have passed since they walked the land. Through the years, mankind has attempted to preserve those venerable sites to enforce and mark its collective memory. For every bitter remembrance that travel brings closer, there are likewise symbols of achievement and accomplishment that point toward a more just and promising future.

The Knowledgeable Traveler's Imprint

A person who travels to places where citizens are repressed or where they have been subject to recent atrocities or serious violations by the government should be aware of such circumstances. Ignorance of the current state of affairs and the recent history which led to it in a location that a person visits is a deficiency; a tourist should be informed. A little reading beforehand, or just keeping up with the news about the destination you journey to is a simple cure for such traveler oversight. I would not recommend going to Chile or to Nicaragua without some idea of what recent decades have inflicted upon the people there, or to Guatemala without knowing about

United States involvement in their Civil War, or Tibet without awareness of the dilemma of the Dalai Lama and the behavior toward the region by the ruling Chinese government. Recent events like the ones that have wracked Myanmar are especially important to know about. A visitor should understandably be expected to be informed about such matters because countries and cultures reflect the history and the experiences and interests of the people one meets. Residents may well bring up in conversation situations which have to do with their lives during such events especially if they involve suffering and trauma. One would do well to have some thoughts and opinions about such current issues as the Israel-Palestinian conflict while traveling in the Middle East or as long-standing and heated a problem as the Armenian question in Turkey. These are matters that people care about in such places and they are topics likely to come up in interactions with the residents who reside in areas involved in such matters. Did you know that there are unresolved border issues due to earlier wars between Chile and Bolivia, Lebanon and Israel, Croatia and Slovenia, India and Pakistan/Nepal/China, Ethiopia and its neighbors and on and on? Perhaps we cannot fathom the implication of these matters in every case but we can enrich our conversations when we go to such places and demonstrate our concerns if we are as well informed visitors as we can possibly be.

Left Hand, Right Hand

There is another more frequently direct and equally important way to express understanding of and identification with the people the traveler meets, a way which is not political but has to do with cultural sensitivity. Tourists should know something about basic local customs and observe simple and visible aspects of cultural practices that are part of the daily way of life where we travel.[22] In today's world, quite a few folks are aware that one does not point his feet at a Muslim with whom one is in conversation because that is considered to be an offensive gesture. Probably most travelers know that we use two kinds of hand signals to display that something is OK, namely, making a fist with the thumb pointed upward or making a circle with the index finger and the thumb. But the fact is that in some Mediterranean areas as well as in several Arab lands, the thumbs up signal is considered an insult. On the other hand, the circle symbol is problematic in several places also including Germany and Brazil; as a matter of fact, it is the equivalent to giving someone the finger here in the States. Even the seemingly harmless V sign which was popularized in Great Britain during WWII becomes a negative in some places when the palm is pointed inward. Using the left hand for eating (It is traditionally employed for toiletry in India and other parts of the Third World) is considered a disgusting behavior in some cultures. Lefties beware! So gestures and other non-verbal practices may convey unwanted or even offensive personal meaning. One should be aware of the most important of these signals before you leave your own

---

22   Head touching, back slapping and looking someone straight in the eye are considered negative behaviors in Southern Asia while these behaviors are very well accepted in most of the West. Personal space varies greatly also as you travel the globe. In Mediterranean countries, if you refrain from touching someone's arm though you know them well when talking to them or if you don't greet them with kisses or a warm embrace, you will be considered cold. But pat the back of someone who is not a family member or a good friend in Korea, and you'll make them uncomfortable. Since hankies are considered inappropriate in certain places, if you are traveling through Eastern and Asian countries, opt for disposable tissues instead. In France as well as in Eastern countries, if you're dining and need to blow your nose, use the restroom or at least turn well away from the table

country and deposit bad feelings elsewhere with unwitting rudeness due to ignorance about the lands to which you travel.

Traveler Manners

One more consideration to be taken into account is simple courtesy, the kind of respect that we should all have for one another regarding privacy and civility, especially when we are visitors whose behavior reflects on all Americans and leaves everything from a good feeling to an unpleasant taste in the mouths of people abroad who witness our actions. There have been several occasions when my pride as a citizen of the United States took a beating because of rudeness on the part of other American travelers. In Puerta Vallarta, for example, I was in line at a restaurant along with quite a few others Americans, many of whom had come on a convenient and inexpensive group trip from Houston. Most of them were drunk, raucous and extremely disrespectful to the staff of the restaurant because there was a long wait for a table. Their behavior marked them clearly as ugly Americans on vacation. I do not spend much time in resorts customarily and I guess one of the reasons for that is the likelihood of crossing paths with people who travel for very different reasons than I do. My feeling was that this occurrence was not especially uncommon at that restaurant. I also recall a time when I went on an adventure trip in India in an area which was surely not a resort. Because we were in the most remote parts of the country, we needed to travel in a small group in order to set up camp where there were no tourist accommodations available. On that trip, I met a man who shared my avid interest in portrait and travel photography who invited me to go with him to take some photos on the street. His wife had told me that he won several prizes for his excellent portraits so I thought I could learn something from him. I did. A woman dressed in the colorful and distinctive dress of the area came walking down the road, a fine subject for our photographic desires indeed. Before I was able to ask her permission to take a few pictures, my companion assaulted her with the camera. Without a word, he just stepped virtually into her path and started shooting photos of her face. If that is how he won his prizes, he was welcome to them. I would have none of that approach. I did not have any desire to spend time with him for any purpose after that incident, and I went about taking my photos my way. I would never push a camera in a subject's face without first engaging that person in conversation and getting permission to take her picture. Nor would I ever want anyone to do such a thing to me. Ugly Americans can be present on all kinds of trips in all kinds of places.

I am quite convinced that politics and Third World travel are deeply interconnected. The choice to visit one particular country or other has many levels. First of all, as I indicated earlier, there is the implicit validation by the traveler of the government of the destination country, its treatment of its citizens and the authenticity of its claims to decency and fairness. Then there is the economic assistance that the visitor provides to the tourism industry wherever he goes. Who gets the money that is brought in and what do they do with it? And finally, there is the opportunity to interact with the people, to bring in news, to spend dollars directly on their behalf, to provide them with fair return for their labor and their craftsmanship, to speak with them about their lives and their government, to inform them about the outside world from which they are sometimes isolated. One cannot always know how these things will manifest themselves during the trip planning stage but the more informed the traveler is, the more impact he can have and the more valuable his travel becomes to the world he journeys through.

CHAPTER EIGHT

BYPRODUCTS

"Travel is more than the seeing of sights; it is a change that goes on, deep and permanent, in the ideas of living."

— Miriam Beard

Given all the joy and knowledge and personal growth that travel in the Third World has provided for me, it is truly amazing to realize that there are also important side benefits in my life, unforeseen bonuses that are directly attributable to this endeavor. The first thing that comes to mind is my children and grandchildren's indication that they would like to follow in my footsteps; they clearly want to see the world much in the way that Bev and I have, and they probably will. My daughter's youngest son, an intrepid traveler who is just nine years old as I write these words, is a true soul mate in this regard as well as in other interests- e.g., photography, museums, peoples and their culture, art, etc. On the wall of my son's former bedroom, there is a large map that papered one entire side of the room. I have taken to putting small round stickers on it to mark places I have visited. My little geographer looked over the map and very quickly let me know that I forgot to mark Swaziland which we had visited on our last family trip. The younger child of my son is equally interested in the world around him so I am certain he will also see a great deal of it. As for my other grandchildren, although the intensity and significance of their respective experiences vary amongst them, they have all been delighted to share their travels and newly acquired knowledge with their classmates in school and they refer frequently to the events which transpired when we were away together. I bring back rocks and foreign currency which a couple of the kids have made collections of. I would have to say that this is the most meaningful and lasting byproduct of my journeys but far from the only one. The fact that my progeny will likely continue such explorations well after I no longer circle the globe puts the explorational aspect of my life in a special category. I suspect my modeling of world travel will influence where and in what way they also wander off the tourist trails.

Getting Smarter

Much of my desire to wander abroad, especially along the less travelled paths, was a yearning to know about others and how they live. Mankind has created a seemingly infinite set of adjustments to the daily needs of living that have challenged people's survival on this earth. Many of these cultural creations are absolutely ingenious and fascinating. Learning about them has been one of the great pleasures of my life. The way that cultures perpetuate their values and history and develop a concept of the world around them from generation to generation is an entire subject in itself. Outside of formal educational systems, dramas, shadow plays, child retreats into woods or caves or other private places with knowledgeable elders, puppetry, story times and innumerable other modes of communication transmit and perpetuate cultural history, mores and attitudes. There are a multitude of ceremonies for practically every life transition which enrich and inform the cultural life of people as well. In West Africa youngsters may be whisked off into the "Sacred Forest" to spend months with the elders of their tribe to receive instruction in how to be a member of the group, tattoos may be inscribed on one or other part of the body to mark a formal transition into a society as is the case in the Sepik Region of Papua New Guinea, girls may have permanent necklaces placed on them like the Padaung people of Southeast Asia or the Bonda tribal women of Eastern India, jewelry or some other decorative objects inserted in their body in places as some peoples do in rural Thailand, Burma or many parts of Africa; boys may have challenges awaiting them where they are required to prove themselves in hunts or in battle or in survival settings before being fully admitted into one or other culture in East Africa or Australia, and so on. Each of these and the multitude of other observances and traditions that exist in various societies around the world are wonderful representations of the variety of adaptations that visitors can witness, especially in the diverse tribal areas of the world.

I have greatly cherished the overall benefits of learning about the history, geography, geology, and general knowledge of the world around me. As I noted earlier, when I hear or read about an international story in the news, I often summon a concrete image or bring to the story a degree of insight about places that would otherwise not be possible. I can picture the markets and the buildings and the locations that are situated at the site of important global events from Tiananmen Square to the city center of Peshawar to the shores of Sumatra or Burma where tsunamis or cyclones have destroyed villages to the great capitols of East and West where important matters and decisions have taken place. The occurrences themselves become virtually palpable to me, the people are familiar and the locales are etched in clarifying context. I can even picture the folks I came to know and interact with at times. A deep enrichment of my understanding of such happenings is the welcome reward I reap for having visited so many of the places I read about. One can never anticipate when images will reappear in one's mind to enhance the present and to deepen understanding. Vivid examples of this phenomenon were the news reports during the spring of 2009 when the Pakistani army was trying to drive the Taliban and other extremists out of the mountainous border area with Afghanistan. The Swat Valley was cited for weeks as the major center of activity. When I was in Pakistan, I drove along the Karakorum Highway and passed through the Swat Valley. I found it to be an incredibly beautiful mountain area but also a region that was quite lawless even then if one left the main road and motored into the hills. We were instructed not to wander from the highway at all. Who could have ever imagined that one day I would be recalling that drive and the little, modest hotel where we stayed, all thanks to the images on TV that kept popping up under our nose? And the photos of the main town along the road through the Swat Valley have been seen by every audience which has viewed my Pakistan slide program for their entertainment.

There are many other instances when I recall travelling through some area, usually one I was quite unfamiliar with prior to my visit, and then subsequently read major news stories about important events that transpired there. It was only about two years after our visit to Chiapas in Mexico that major opposition protests in that region threatened the stability and viability of the central government of Mexico itself. The Tsunami that killed so many innocents in Southern Asia and did so much damage to the islands of Sumatra in Indonesia and Phuket in Thailand followed our visits to those areas several years later; we walked the beaches where the catastrophe occurred and were in some of the towns that were washed away. As we were visiting the Philippines, papers were reporting on the activities of the terrorists there in the Southern Islands, an insurrection that continued for many years after our visit. Tiananmen Square is especially dramatic for us because of the historic happenings that occurred after we were there. It was an extraordinary aftermath to the visit we remembered so well. We stayed in the Taj Mahal Hotel in Mumbai a couple of times and were in the very building where the bombings occurred that shook the government of India and deepened their distrust of Pakistan just a couple of years later. I could go on but these happenings and the news they generated had special meaning for us and still does. This is just one more way our world has been enriched unexpectedly and deepened considerably. Uygur terrorists, Peshawar, Beijing, Karachi, Katmandu, San Sebastian, Gaza, Yangon, Sri Lanka, and countless other places are not just names; they are memories and images that are fixed in my mind.

Reading Unfamiliar Authors

There is another intellectual pleasure that has expanded for me which is largely ascribable to my travel, namely, the joy and knowledge I have gained from reading both fiction and non-fiction (especially the latter) from recent and contemporary foreign authors whose guidance I sought in order to understand more deeply the cultures of the their respective countries. Carlos Fuentes from Mexico, Mario Vargas Llosa from Peru, Jorge Amado, whose tales of the State of Bahia in Brazil markedly enriched my travel to that part of the world and whose stories were consistently entertaining, Isabel Allende from Chile, Jorge Luis Borges, the Argentine, whose work is probably the most famous in South America, and of course, the father of Magical Realism, Gabriel Garcia Marquez, born in Columbia, whose *One Hundred Years of Solitude* and *Love in the Time of Cholera* are two of the most important books of the last century written anywhere and among my very favorites pieces of literature. These are just a few of the authors who accompanied me through the cultures and politics and history of lands south of our border and who greatly augmented my understanding of that part of the world.

I am already relatively familiar with European authors but I knew little about the best writers in Asia and Africa until I traveled to those areas. My favorite book from West Africa is *Things Fall Apart* by Chinua Achebe of Nigeria whose entire trilogy was outstanding. West Africa has produced another prize winning and world class novelist in Wole Soyinka as well as other authors. Egyptian literature has been especially outstanding of late featuring the works of still another Nobel Prize winning author who died recently, Naguib Mahfouz. His *Cairo Trilogy* was a brilliant piece of writing which I could barely put down until I finished all three books. *The Children of Gabalawi* also known as *The Children of the Street* was my most recent Mahfouz read and one more fascinating story written by this courageous and talented author. Mahfouz has taught me much about the daily life that flourishes in the alleys of Cairo. Alaa Al Aswany is another Egyptian whose work I enjoy, especially his book, *The Yacoubian Building,* a rather tongue in cheek picture of modern Egypt which I read during my recent trip to that country. Although it was written quite a while ago, I think my favorite reading of the last decade is the inspiring novel from South Africa, *The Power of One,* by Bryce Courtenay. Among other outstanding authors from that land are Nadine Gordimer and J.M. Coetzee, both Nobel Prize winners and documentarians of their country, its nature and its history.

In India, the production of worthwhile books, most of which are written in English, becomes enough in itself to fill one's reading list and provides an enormous amount of information about that country. Some Indian authors are recent immigrants to America or England and, while they may have fully adopted their new lands, they constantly refer back to their homeland as a source for their writing. Salman Rushdie is probably the most famous writer in the world since the Fatwa was issued for his life, but he and other wonderful story tellers help the reader decipher the mysteries of that exotic land as well as provide endless delight. R. K. Narayan is one of my favorites; I have also enjoyed Jhumpa Lahiri, Amitav Ghosh, Anita Desai, among others. I could go on and on about the authors I have come to know from travel but the point is that they have substantially contributed to the insights I have gained in my travels and greatly enriched the breadth of my reading choices.

Sharing the Trips

Then there are the highly personal matters that I would call my idiosyncratic benefits. One of these is the development of a post-retirement travel lecture program which has become an essential, productive part of my life. I have always taken photos of my travels (more about this below) and I began to utilize much more broadly my collection of pictures and stories and information about each journey after I left a lifelong career of teaching and educational administration. Shortly after retirement, I began to market cultural presentations to libraries, schools, retirement communities, colleges, clubs and other such venues. It took me a while to master the marketing process itself, yet another story and another challenge entirely, but that paid off greatly because, in spite of modest earnings from this endeavor, my interest and pleasure in sharing where I have been and what it is like to travel to those places, most of which are unfamiliar to my audiences, have been quite rewarding. My programs are appreciated by the people who attend them and presenting them has been an extension of what I long ago came to love most of all - teaching. The difference is that now I am always teaching something I care very much about and with which I have intimate personal experience and I choose to do this at the level I desire and at the times I prefer. I especially enjoy teaching classes at universities and other such places whenever possible so that I can more thoroughly cover a geographical area. The opportunity to work with people of all ages, not just junior and senior high school students as I formerly did, has also enriched my retirement. I have always enjoyed doing new things. While I was still working as a full time educator, I did occasionally give similar presentations, but only for my friends whom I had to bribe with dinner or my students at school as part of my teaching function. It is nice to get paid now for showing them to interested audiences and it is especially rewarding to get applause at the end of a program. Who would have thought this extension of an earlier enjoyable career would also become a byproduct of my travel? I should mention here that many tourists now blog their friends from exciting (and also from boring) trips now that technology has enabled such instant transmission of experiences. I recently began to send my friends a summary over the internet toward the end of each of our journeys.

Cruising Along

Although it did not become a highly valued product of my travel, there has been another quite unexpected and positive outcome from my presentations which I enjoyed several times over the past years also. I mentioned earlier that I contacted one of the high quality luxury cruise lines some years after I was well into my Third World adventures and I was employed by the company as a lecturer on Mediterranean, Black Sea and North Sea Cruises. My work involved doing presentations about the destinations which were stops on the cruises. That opportunity enabled me to revisit many places I had gone to earlier in my travels and to do so at little expense as well as to explore some European sites I had missed. Both our transportation to the ships and our stay on them were completely free. I enjoyed those trips and felt quite appreciated by the audiences. Nonetheless, I ultimately discontinued working on the ships because I eventually decided that cruising the customary sea routes is less rewarding than my usual style of independent, leisurely and more challenging voyaging. As a matter of fact, I would probably have never ventured onto a cruise ship had I not been offered the opportunity to go virtually free on one of the most luxurious ships on the sea. The cruises I signed onto were incredibly well-appointed (I do not usually travel that way), cost virtually nothing, and took us back to places I probably would never have otherwise returned. I managed also to get to see a number of Mediterranean sites that I would never have visited had I not been a cruise passenger. In the back of my mind I always had a notion to visit the Greek Islands and I had never really spent enough time along the beautiful coastlines of the Mediterranean earlier. I was happy I had a chance to do so. The effort the ships required from me was minimal and the rewards were truly impressive. A revisit to some of my favorite spots like Istanbul, Rome, Venice, Barcelona and others were part of the benefits. Stops along the Black Sea and a return to the Scandinavian capitals were also quite interesting. It was not Third World travel but no complaints here. It was novel, edifying and enjoyable for the most part nonetheless. On the voyages I met folks I would customarily never have had the opportunity to rub elbows with, multi-millionaires who were far more used to the indulgences I encountered on board than I was. I even had dinner with former president Habibi of Indonesia, the third person to rule that country, on one trip and was presented with a gift of his photography from him after our meal. As you can imagine, we had an interesting conversation over dinner. I sailed in the region at the same time the euro was soaring in value against the dollar. I know that our comfortable return to favorite locales would never have happened were that not the case. There were many other cruising opportunities offered in subsequent years but I had either spent sufficient time at the scheduled ports on the itinerary of the ship or there was too much time on the sea. There were even Third World cruises I considered but the idea of flying to Asia and spending so much of our time cruising the seas and so little in the ports where ships stop was simply not inviting enough. The chance to go on such cruises was a clear byproduct of the programs I developed about my most remote, intensive and intimate journeys, some of which turned out to be desired presentations even for the comfort oriented travelers on the luxury ship.

Photography

The emergence of my photography as a serious hobby and a significant part of my life has been perhaps the single most important spinoff from travel however. I had always taken photos on trips as I indicated earlier and I received many complements from friends for my ability to capture attractive illustrations for the stories of our journeys that I related to them. One woman who saw some photos I had printed as I picked them up in our neighborhood camera store admired them and suggested that I join the camera club she belonged to in the nearby suburbs of Philadelphia. I was flattered by her comments so I went to a meeting and entered a competition. I had such beginner's luck on that first visit that it made me think I might have talent with a camera. I joined the club and have been a participant ever since. It was through the competitions and lectures there and in other related settings I sought out that I really did begin to improve in the technical aspects of photography about which I formerly knew very little. I have even had a couple of successful photo shows along the way. Although I am still very much an amateur and feel somewhat limited in the many details and skills that contribute to effective use of a camera, I have been able to enter many contests over the past ten or so years and I have won quite a few prizes competing with folks who have been devoted to the art for much longer than I and who approach it in a far more serious way. I probably take about one tenth of the photos on a given day of travel than many of the contestants I vie with since it is travel itself that remains my most important focus. You can view some of this photography at my website: www.travellectures.com. I am still primarily a travel photographer but my interest is becoming broader and deeper than just recording travel experiences. I have progressed to processing images creatively, I appreciate more deeply the work of others in many areas of photography and I do use my camera in places other than the Third World. The hobby has become an ever growing additional focus of interest and pleasure for me. As I have approached photography more seriously, I find that I now notice things I never looked at carefully before. It had been a cyclical development for me to learn to take better images and then have the taking of them increase my ability to view what I am looking at more deeply. And I do not mean just when I travel. I now note more fully the texture and shapes of the trees and the patterns of shade while bicycling along a riverside and I observe more intensely the colors in the sky at dusk. These observations enrich my day wherever and however they take place. What a joy it is to have this kind of development appear and grow and contribute to my retirement years!

Our Museum of Memorabilia

As I roamed through the Third World, it took very little time to discover the economic advantages in the destination countries for those who arrived with dollars in their pockets. That benefited us considerably in that we could usually get cheaper hotels, food, and commodities than we would have been able to in more developed areas. It especially enabled us to buy local crafts to an extent I could never have done in the West. So long as I stayed away from gold and precious stones (no problem for us at all), I was able to indulge my fascination with the craftsmanship I encountered in places like India, Indonesia, Southeast Asia, Africa and Latin America, the South Pacific and other locales. Sadly though, that state of affairs exists primarily because of the low reimbursement that craft persons receive for their time and talent in such places. A beautiful weaving in the market in Tarabuco, Bolivia or Otovalo, Ecuador which might well have taken the creator a week or two or even more time can likely be had for as little as $30.00 or less. An equivalent object in the United States, an Indian carving in Santa Fe for example, would likely cost well into the hundreds of dollars. Silver jewelry from India embedded with semi-precious stones costs little more than the weight of the silver which itself also happens to be cheaper in India, the small price of the stones plus just a couple of rupees for the spectacular and often painstaking handiwork that someone had invested in the piece. What might cost several hundred dollars in the States could be had for a fraction of that amount from a vendor or small store keeper in the Third World. While I bemoan the disparity of wages throughout the world and support as many efforts as I can to rectify that inequity, the point is that the discrepancy in price enabled us (and still does in many places) to bring home fascinating items, a collection striking enough for folks to refer to our home as a museum. Our walls are filled with batiks from Africa and Bali, weavings from Mexico, Peru, Laos, Vietnam, Myanmar and Indonesian islands, and

Thangkas[23] from Nepal and India. On our shelves stand interesting items from Batak writings on bark to lost-wax method metalwork from West Africa to sandalwood or traditional, unique metal tribal statuary from Nepal and India. Our trips surround us in the form of these memorabilia and make our home an interesting place to just roam through according to our visitors.

I do want to note, however that, wherever and whenever possible, we shop at local cooperatives that have been organized throughout the Third World to help artisans get a fair return for their labor. These are growing enterprises and offer promise for the future of such commerce. We were delighted to find such institutions as far away from one another as the Island of Tequila in Lake Titicaca, Peru and a village in the heart of Lombok, Indonesia. Organizations exist to support socially positive developments like equal pay for goods from *FINCA*, an NGO that provides small loans and related financial services to budding farmers and vendors in poverty settings so that they can begin small businesses to *Ten Thousand Villages*, a trade organization which supports fair pricing for crafts persons throughout the Third World as well as eco-sustainable products. There are also very localized organizations dedicated to one particular area or tribal group as well. *Kallari*, for example, is a cooperative based in London which supports cultural groups in the Amazon by helping to sell sustainable crafts indigenous to that area. There are innumerable such outfits on the internet for those interested in helping poor people

23   A thangka (sometime spelled Tanka) is a pictorial representation either embroidered or painted and includes some aspect of the life of Buddha or other devotional figure or design which can be used for prayer in homes or temples. These are also used as meditational objects to further personal enlightenment. They are popular items in both Nepal and Tibet. For Buddhists, these objects are considered to be beautiful aspects of the divine and are stimulating representations of their beliefs.

economically which enable the contributor to select a geographical area or a tribal group or women or other subgroup they may have a special interest in.

My primary incentive for purchasing items even now that our house has no room for further display is my use of artifacts in the presentations I give. One of the things that my audiences really enjoy is seeing and hearing about the crafts and other artifacts of the culture I am presenting a program about. I pass around many of these to enhance the enjoyment of those who attend my lectures as well as to provide them a tangible contact with the place I am discussing. A cassowary knife[24] used for scarring the back of a young person during an initiation ceremony, an Indonesian Batak tribal calendar written on a piece of bark indigenous to Sumatra, a weight used to measure gold in West Africa or a camel tooth necklace made by the Tuareg of Mali all help to enrich the stories I tell and the photos I show and make for an even more engrossing evening of presentation. Some of the artifacts themselves are instructive. When I describe the complicated and extensive process developed in Burma for preparing the gold leaf to put on the statues of the Buddha, I am talking about the creativity and history of the people themselves. It is rewarding to observe the enjoyment that folks experience in handling rare and integral objects of a cultural area. As the people often say to me at the end of a lecture, "Now I don't have to go there." For some, that is neither true nor is it a positive way of thinking though it may well be accurate for them. There are many, because of age or means or physical condition, for whom it is a statement of fact. At any rate, it is quite

---

24   A cassowary knife is made from the thighbone of the cassowary bird, a large, flightless animal (actually the largest land animal in Papua New Guinea.) These knives are common in the jungle area and may be used for hunting, fighting or ceremonies. They are often decorated with clay and/or feathers. They are fascinating artifacts.

satisfying to bring people closer to appreciating and learning about ways of life so uncommon and different from their own, realities they may never have otherwise known about or imagined.

Many of the items from our travels are quite special on their own merits aside from their function as memorabilia for us or information for my audiences. Even if they were bought in a specialty store without reference to their source, they would be worthy of admiration either because of their rarity or the incredible workmanship they represent. Perhaps my very favorite artifact is a 10 inch high figure of an elephant I purchased in Srinigar, Kashmir many years ago at a little shop just off one of the many small canals that intersect the city. It is created primarily from paper mache which is lacquered and then very finely decorated in gold paint with a delicate rat's tail. It is an exceptionally finely worked piece of craftsmanship that is simply lovely to look at and is reminiscent of the kind of detailed Muslim workmanship that has characterized that area for hundreds of years. Many years ago I invested $150.00 on this item out of a souvenir budget of about $500.00 which we had designated for the purchase of artifacts on a lengthy Asian trip. Although we bought that elephant during the very first week of the trip, we have never regretted this early purchase. Another item which jumps out in my mind is a beautiful and extremely delicate carving from the Philippines. It consists of several figures intertwined and free-floating but created from a single piece of local and rare hardwood. It took a meticulous, skilled Ifugao workman in the northernmost reach of Luzon to create that object. One slip and perhaps a week or more of work was down the drain. In travel to the tribal areas of India, I have brought back several of my favorite creations consisting of poured metal figures representing fanciful and spiritual handiwork that are probably as good examples of traditional art as can be found anywhere. It is their imagination and originality that are the most appealing aspects of the figures, however, so their function and relationship to our travel which we value so much are not at all necessary for someone else to appreciate them. There are other objects, too many to list here, which are just items of beauty or inspirational in their concept or workmanship. They all capture the viewer's eye and none of them broke the bank. The most dramatic object of all sits right in the middle of the floor of our living room and cannot be missed as you enter my house; it is a tribal rug from Iran which we bought in Peshawar on our visit to Pakistan. I well remember the conversation the day we bought it. First of all, the idea of purchasing an oriental rug in that country was something we had considered before we went on that trip; although we did not possess a great deal of knowledge about oriental rugs. We did do a bit of research before we left the States so we would be decently prepared should an occasion present itself, and we felt that Pakistan might be the right place to find one we liked if it fit our interests and was the right price. Our guide in Peshawar asked us if we wanted to see any rugs during one of our days exploring the city.

Not really.

(We were reluctant to spend the time necessary for shopping)

You don't have to buy anything and you might be interested in how they are made.

If we pass a store that looks interesting, perhaps we will take a look.

(Ten minutes of driving later)

How about this shop?

Let's try it.

(We enter and are greeted by the owner, a pudgy, well-spoken fellow) Hello, my friends. Are you interested in a rug?

We really don't want to buy a rug but we will look around.

(Good bargaining posture we surmised)
No problem. Have a seat. Would you like some tea?
No. Thanks. We can't spend too much time here.
(Tea and candies arrive nonetheless)
It is my obligation to serve our guests. Let me show you a few rugs anyhow. Do you have a preference about the type or color or size?
Not really. The size would have to fit our living room though, about 8x10 feet.
(One of four men drags a rug to the middle of the floor)
Do you like this rug?
No. That kind of repeated geometric pattern does not appeal to us.
(Another rug is laid on top of the first)
How about this one? Which do you prefer?
We don't know that we want any but the second is a bit more appealing.
(Process continues and dozens of rugs come out for examination each placed on top of the last creating a small additional Pakistani mountain. Tea and soda and sweets follow again. After the workers carry out one carpet after another, we finally see one which we do like, the one we ultimately bought. We narrow the choice down to two possibilities and then finally to the one we like best)
How much would this rug cost?
Business is very slow and you are our first customer of the day.
(We had that distinction many times in our travel)
For you, we would sell this rug for $2800.00.
Oh, my goodness. Thank you but we would not spend any more than $1000.00 although we are sure that your price is a very fair one. Let us think about it. We have a couple of more days in Peshawar.

(We actually were considering spending a bit more than a thousand dollars to replace a bare and faded inexpensive rug we had for many years)

My friends, let us sit down, have a bit more tea together and I will make a bargain for you, for our special American guests. What would be your best price?

We have budgeted $1000.00 but we could go a little bit higher, perhaps. What is your best price?

This is a rare carpet, one you could not get in America for twice the price I am asking. At $2500.00 it would be a steal for you. Can we agree on an acceptable price today? If you buy it now, I will make you a very special offer.

And what would that be?

Let us say $2300.00 and shake hands on that.

It is still far too much beyond our means. We will pay you $1500.00 but we won't go any higher.

I am afraid I cannot sell it to you at that price. We cannot get these rugs because they are not weaving them any longer in Iran. I will let you have it for $2000.00. Final offer.

We finally settled on the lovely Afghan tribal rug at $1800.00 stretching ourselves more than we originally intended to and we had it sent to our home. It arrived about six weeks or so after we returned in quite good condition. After I picked it up at customs, got it into the house and unrolled it on our floor though, it turned out to be 9' by 13'. The rug was much larger than I indicated we had room for to the shopkeeper. Luckily, we were able to fit it in the room and it is a spectacular sight to behold. It is the prettiest oriental rug I can imagine. We later discovered that the actual value of an equivalent carpet at a shop in the United States would be about $6000.00 so we actually did get a bargain. That plus the memory of the experience of the sale make the rug a great value to us. I am just glad it fits in our living room. Another Third World adventure – this time in shopping.

Collecting

Bev and I have enjoyed surrounding ourselves with reminders of the trips we go on and have each developed a focus to our shopping. For her, the many forms and shapes and materials that folks use to create necklaces have been an inviting collecting specialty. Since necklaces are a rather ubiquitous artifact, it works out for her wherever we go. She has several dozen or more interesting pieces of neckwear from the carved wooden animal necklaces I talked about earlier which are made in Tanzania and Kenya and South Africa to intricately worked silver necklaces from all over India, Nepal and North Africa including those of several tribal groups. There are outstanding silver and jeweled pieces from Afghanistan and Pakistan especially as well as fine pieces of jade from Mexico and bone or old ivory from China and Thailand. She often has the pleasure of wearing her trip reminders when we go out. You might say we take our trips everywhere with us. The average price of these artifacts is probably less than $20 to $40 apiece with some of them costing only a few dollars and the best valued at as much as $150. But the most important aspect of the necklaces is the handiwork and what the item says about the cultural area where it was purchased.

For me, the collector's choice are masks. I actually bought my first mask on the streets of Paris in 1958. I purchased it simply because the carving pleased me very much aesthetically. The vendor told me it came from Zaire, the country which is now named the Democratic Republic of the Congo. I knew nothing about masks at the time (and not much more about what was earlier called Zaire) so I took him at his word and brought it back with me from my teaching sojourn in Europe. The source was not a significant issue for me at the time. I still enjoy the mask as a piece of art yet it was not until almost 40 years later when I went first to Indonesia and later to New Guinea and West Africa that I added significantly to what has ultimately become a meaningful personal collection. Before the Indonesian trip, I had accumulated another couple of masks on journeys but again only because I liked the look of them and because I was discovering that masks were an excellent illustration of cultural beliefs and local craftsmanship. They were slowly developing into the best reminders of where I had been so all of the rest of my mask collection was bought right where I traveled or quite nearby. I had found my perfect tourist memento. Each one of the faces which looks out from my wall tells a story. There are depictions of birds and crocodiles on some whose symbolism is valued greatly by the people who carved them. There are spirit faces and fearful figures meant to protect the residents of the house where they stood in their native villages. There are smiling lips and protruding eyes that paraded in church processions as well as powerful images of gods from temple Pujahs or ceremonial parades in Sri Lanka and India and Bali. Some masks come from the Spirit Houses of Sepik River villages in Papua New Guinea. Others are simply decorative and were used for events like Carnival parades in Brazil or Mexico. Some are distinctively crafted by small tribal groups in South or Central America; others are meant to represent characters in Chinese opera; and still others were constructed for magical ceremonies of voodoo or objects used as fetishes.

Over the years, I have learned a great deal about masks and their meanings. I pored over books and other sources which explain the wooden and metal images I gaze on in my dining room and along my halls. Through those readings I have come to admire and understand more fully the art and the representations that each of those objects stands for. Some of the nuances - combinations of animal representations, varied materials chosen for the construction of the mask, and characteristics which are typical of one region or another - have enabled me to become reasonably knowledgeable about the art form. While I am surely no expert, I can appreciate more fully true excellence in mask making and can frequently identify the tribal group that created them. That has been another enjoyable byproduct of my travel experiences. On my website, I have posted a few of those masks and subsequently interacted with others who share my interest in mask collecting. I have even been able to provide a few helpful responses to inquiries received from contacts on the net about where a mask the questioner owns originated and even occasionally what it represents. It is always nice to have additional knowledge about the world around you. I find that makes life more interesting. I guess I am truly a mask collector now.

All of this collecting helped to provide more adventure and enrichment along our journeys. I remember a few places I would just never have stopped had I not had an interest in adding to the kinds of objects I found appealing to bring back with us. When I am with a guide, I usually make him or her aware that masks are a special interest of mine and that I would be quite happy to find a mask maker or a store which specializes in that particular craft. Because of that I have discovered several engaging and talented craftsmen and have bought a couple of attractive and rare pieces that I love to look at. I mentioned earlier a houseboat trip up the Mahakam River in Borneo (Kalimantan, Indonesia). That was one of the times I told a guide about my mask collection. He did not respond but he surely listened. A day or two into the trip, our boat just pulled up to a tiny village at the side of the river where I disembarked and followed the guide up the dirt path that led along the riverside. After a quarter mile walk, he introduced us to a mask maker working in a rattan and wood shack between the road and the river. It turned out that the man was a specialist in a kind of mask that was only used in that part of Borneo. It was a dance mask designed for a particular ceremony that takes place just once a year, roughly equivalent to their celebration of the beginning of the new year. He had actually just finished constructing a beautiful example of that type of mask which included brass earrings like the women in the area typically wore, mirrors inside the wooden eye sockets he had fashioned, chains of locally made beads and other colorful decorations. I loved it and knew instantly that I wanted it. But - it was not for sale. The proprietor explained that I could buy one of the older, mustier masks on his wall which he just happened to have left over from previous ceremonies. Although they may have been more valuable to collectors, I did not find them especially attractive so I asked how much the new one would be if it were for sale. Thirty dollars was the reply, an amount he apparently did not think anyone would pay for his handiwork. The mask now hangs prominently on the wall of our foyer greeting all visitors who enter. I did not even try to bargain on that occasion. It is indeed one of my favorites. Incidentally, because someone had looked at my page of masks in my website, I was contacted with an offer to buy a similar mask the person wanted to sell. The asking price - $1500.00. That was not my first sticker shock, by the way. In the Soho district of New York City, I stumbled into a store that specialized in New Guinean artifacts and discovered that the equivalent cost for items compared to what I had paid was about 5 or 10 to one. A similar experience took place on another New York City stroll although it was not a mask in question on that occasion. I passed a stall in Greenwich Village which featured some West African artifacts. To my great surprise, there was a necklace (Bev's specialty) on sale which featured a simple bronze wheel design attached to a leather strap. It was identical to one I had bought in the Dogon area of Mali some years earlier. I remembered bargaining with the man who offered the necklace and was told by him that the bronze piece had been found in the caves where the Dogon tribe had settled when they arrived in the area and was produced by a people called the Tellum who lived there before the Dogon displaced or absorbed them at the end of the eighteenth century and of whom few traces remained. I was unable to discern whether that was true or not but the bronze necklace looked like a museum piece so I invested in it for the price we agreed upon. At any rate, when I saw what appeared to be a duplicate piece for sale along the street, I was curious. The man who was selling it said he did not know where it came from but he said he would sell it to me for a good price. When he said seven fifty, I responded that I paid seventeen fifty for the one I had bought in Mali and then carried it back with me. I got cheated, I muttered. I paid $17.50 and you are offering it to me for $7.50. No, said he, I mean seven hundred and fifty dollars, not seven dollars and fifty cents. My jaw dropped. I doubt I will ever know if I got cheated in Mali but I do know I could have gotten more than $7.50 for the necklace from that artifact salesman. Another bargain and another surprise.

Two more mask stories. One of my favorite items is called a Gable Mask, an oversized creation meant to be placed above the door of a spirit house in a Papua New Guinea jungle village. The mask sits at the top of the stairway leading to the second floor from our foyer where it has peered down on us for over fourteen years. It is a gruesome looking apparition made entirely of vines, large nuts and other natural items from the Sepik Forest. Its purpose is to keep evil spirits out of the building upon which it is placed. I love the mask for its unique appearance and construction and for a number of other reasons including the fact that it is about four feet high and I carried it in a black plastic garbage bag for three weeks of active travel before I arrived back home. But the most important thing about it is that, since it was placed on the wall facing our stairway, not a single evil spirit has ascended those steps. What a functional piece of art! I do not spend an enormous amount of money on our travel purchases but I do seem to get a bang for the buck nonetheless. Another mask I admired very much was on the wall of the Karawari Lodge, also in the Sepik area. (The villages of PNG are wonderful locales for the fabrication of traditional art in many forms.) It was also a somewhat oversized creation and extremely well crafted. I was looking at it longingly when Bev said she would leave me if I bought one more big mask like that. After she left to return to our room, I paid for the mask and arranged to have it sent to our house. (There was no way I could carry it with me anyhow.) It arrived at our door about a month or so after we returned from PNG. I was home alone when it arrived so I unwrapped it, put it on a chair facing the door, and told Bev later on that we had a surprise visitor. She took one look at the mask and screamed. Her surprise turned into laughter, thankfully, partly because of what I had done, but also because she realized I could not resist any mask I fell in love with. It sits today right in the center of the wall in our dining room surrounded by a host of other lovely representations of spirits and images and it stands out even in that setting. It is truly a dazzling piece of traditional art.

I appreciate deeply what Third World travel brought into my life. We each connect to the world in a distinctive, idiosyncratic way. If I had all of my travel still before me, I am sure my own journeys and experiences would be different from the ones I actually went on since time and circumstance are immeasurable variables. But everyone brings a unique set of inclinations and preferences to every undertaking. Another traveler would likely collect objects that reflect far different interests or a completely contrary intensity. Still other folks might focus on animals or birds or buildings or art or religion encountered in the places where they journey. Hobbies and interests accompany one on every journey and help to modify one's focus and decision making. One can chose to learn traditional weaving from craft persons whose families have been engaged in that undertaking for generations in the hill towns of Bolivia or Laos. Musicians can bring back traditional instruments or time-honored melodies or songs from practically every locale in the Third World. Artists can explore new styles or weave traditional themes into their work from almost every culture they visit. Herbal gardening, various meditation techniques, alternative health treatments, dance movements and other such potential focuses are abundant in the places I travel. There is an endless possibility of variations which enable someone to build upon whatever their interests were before their journeys. That is another wonderful thing about peering into the byways of the world; we all notice something just a bit different from the next person gazing at the same scene.

I do not know how many hundreds of folks have entered our home since I started my travels – friends, vendors, people arriving for meetings or parties in our living room, workmen, family members, etc. – but few of them fail to be captured by the masks and batiks and paintings on the walls, the curiosities from strange places on just about every available surface, the carvings and pottery and figures from all over the world. The conversations stimulated by these objects offer me a chance to share how meaningful the items are to me and where and how they had been gathered. Curious visitors ask question after question about my travel, about the meaning of some object, about my personal reaction to one artifact or other. So our knick-knacks are also conversation starters, pieces of information for others, and decorative additions to the museum I call my home. I view all of this as one more bonus of my travel experience which never diminishes, continually gives me pleasure and reminds me how lucky I have been. Of course, there is a downside to just about everything I suppose. I cannot imagine how I could ever move out of the house I live in. An apartment or smaller home would never accommodate the many memories represented in every corner of our current home. And how could I ever part with objects which are living memories for us? Even years later, I remember where each one was purchased. I recall as well what one item or another meant in the culture where it was produced. I remember the bargaining at stalls or the lucky circumstance that enabled me to find an out of the way place in some dusty village where a treasure (at least in my opinion) sat on a shelf waiting for just the right visitor to arrive. I acquired just about every single item you would encounter in our house from my travels. My entire home is one ongoing flow of memories.

CHAPTER NINE

NOTHING LASTS FOREVER

"Twenty years from now you will be more disappointed by the things that you didn't do than by the ones you did do. So throw off the bowlines. Sail away from the safe harbor. Catch the trade winds in your sails. Explore. Dream. Discover."

— Mark Twain

Bev was reminiscing about her life the other day and stated that, if she were asked if there was anything she desired to do before her days were over, her answer would be that she had basically done all the things she wanted to do in a very rich lifetime. Our opinions coincide in that respect. Some folks dream that they want to see some of "the world" before they leave it; we have already managed to travel to most of the places we desired to visit. How fortunate can anyone be? Given the presence of lots of love and wonderful people surrounding us much of the time (the folks we have enjoyed most sharing our joys of adventure with), there is little to wish for. Touring the world has just been a gift and a pleasure, as well as an achievement.

At the same time, if one does not make a conscious effort to augment his or her life with a firm commitment to adventure and travel, the potential riches of the journey are not likely to occur. Later on, as a time line, just does not cut it. I encourage the dreamer to get going as early as possible and not take too many extensive rest stops along the way. I remember a day many years ago in the middle of my career when a representative of a tax shelter program came to my workplace to sell me his policy. He explained in great detail that the earlier I began and the more money I put into the program (of course, he suggested investing the maximum), the earlier I would be able to retire and the more comfortable I would be some thirty or so years down the road. At one level, that made sense but the implications of following his advice had a drawback of considerable proportion. I thought hard about the option he recommended and decided that I did not want to save the maximum amount of money I could but would rather put away a reasonable amount of my salary, tighten my belt in certain aspects of daily life and use the rest of my income to enrich our recreation and travel. Bev, who was also a teacher at the time, did the same thing. We sheltered less than some other folks we know decided to but we also managed to take enjoyable, modest trips each year, usually a short journey over our winter breaks and a more extensive one in the summer. We looked forward to each of these anticipated highlights as well as toward building a satisfactory foundation for our retirement. If we had to work an extra year or so to make that happen, so be it. The balance we reached between these competing priorities has served us well.

The alternative, namely saving money in order to begin dream journeys at some indefinite point after retirement is that there are no guarantees that one will be in a position to do so physically when that time comes around. I have been lucky enough to have sixteen productive years from the time my work ended until I began to write this book, during which time I have been in rather good health and was able to roam the world at my leisure with far less concern about cost than I had years earlier. (You know the quip about getting on the road after the kids leave the home, the dog dies and the house is paid off. That turned out to be accurate for us.) It has been a wonderful period of our lives. The fact that our health has been good, a requirement for even easy, adventurous travel, was another very lucky circumstance in our lives. But that care free time is now substantially modified. Medical problems have reduced my energy of late and altered my assumption that we could go anywhere we wanted without excessive concern about the availability of medical services or about my ability to be mobile enough to walk or climb to the places I most wanted to see. My walking has slowed, my bodily needs have increased, and my destinations have become correspondingly more limited. That is what happens to most people at some time in their lives, some far earlier than others. I have no complaints about this development because we did do all that we could when we could and that is the best anyone can ask for.

A New Ball Game

When we left for Egypt recently, it was with questions I had never before asked in preparation for a trip. Since I was unable to walk long distances, what would the availability of wheelchairs be at the sites in the areas we were to explore? We were informed that it was not very common for them to be accessible, especially on the paths to the pyramids and at many of the most in interesting temples. I imagined I would have to use camels for transport in some of those places, or maybe even mules. I anticipated I would not be able to do my usual thing which has been to visit just about every desirable point of interest. That prospect was a new challenge to me but other travelers do not necessarily choose to explore every single site they are within reach of so I pictured myself joining visitors lolling at the fringes of the temple grounds. Even if I made it to the important monuments, I doubted I would be able to climb inside to the tomb areas or make it up every sandy path to the entranceways. I imagined that I might likely have a few subsequent travel experiences after the Egypt sojourn but that they would just not be quite as rewarding or comprehensive as my earlier ones. As it turned out, my concerns were resolved by the availability of a wheelchair on the small ship we cruised the Nile on and at many of the temples I wanted to access. A sailor from the ship accompanied us and pushed me along in the chair wherever I needed assistance; we paid this helpful young man a gratuity which did not overly tax our budget and satisfied him quite adequately. I got to see most of the places I wanted to visit and my trip turned out to be a full and rewarding one.

On the trip to Egypt I also needed to make sure I had all my pills and medical information with me but that has been an increasingly important requirement for my travel over the past couple of years. The list of pills I carry in my toilet article bag increases annually. I also now have to be more careful of infection than I was earlier. That is one more worry about something I rarely paid much attention to even in the most remote of locations. I will probably need to know where good doctors are located on any future trips should some unexpected problem arise due to my medical vulnerabilities. These are all matters that were never part of my consideration as I traveled during the past decades. What that all means is that I was quite free, not only to choose the places I was going to, but that I was also able to give my full concentration to matters I really wanted to focus on such as the sites I wanted to see, my priorities after I arrived at my destination, and the exploration of whatever adventures lay ahead of me. Thinking about one's bodily needs or susceptibilities detracts greatly from the joy and the intensity of a journey. But the correlation between anxiety and reality is not always high. I was at a doctor's office not too long ago for a procedure. The physician who was treating me was a relatively young man in apparent good health. I mentioned to him on an earlier visit that I was planning a trip to South Africa a month or two after the treatment; he presumably envied my plans and delighted in hearing about my upcoming journey and the places I described to him. In the course of the conversation, he mentioned he had arranged accommodations for himself and his family in Punta Cana in the Dominican Republic during a future vacation time. His destination was a self-contained beach resort like most of the accommodations located on the shores of the island. He then explained that he was concerned about one problem however. He heard that it was dangerous to walk out of the location so he was glad that everything was provided for the guests there and that he would not have to undertake any dangerous trips from the resort. He wanted to know if I thought he and his family would be safe,. I am aware that many people think that way but I was nonetheless surprised by his trepidation and the contrast between his vicarious excitement hearing about my intentions to seek adventure in South Africa and the fearfulness he was expressing about his own upcoming, highly circumscribed and protected vacation. Have a pleasant trip, Doc. Just don't assume you have actually visited the Dominican Republic.

Egypt had not been easy for me although I was glad I had gone there. The next challenge I faced was negotiating the trip to South Africa mentioned earlier which I went on with my children and grandchildren. My illness made me a little apprehensive about the upcoming journey though good medical practice is available in most sections of the country. I just did not know if I had the energy or strength to roam so far and to endure some of challenges I would likely face along the way. But my grandchildren were so excited about the trip and about the prospect of an adventure we could all have together in South Africa that I could not bring myself to cancel what I considered to be an unpredictable undertaking. By the time I seriously considered the possible advantages of cancellation, I had already paid substantially all the costs for what would be our most expensive vacation ever. I would have gotten a partial refund back from travel insurance but not all the money I put down, So we went.

Although I felt like a patient some of the time, resting more than the others or being pushed in a wheelchair at several sites by my children and grandchildren to keep me from getting too tired, I was happy that I decided to go ahead with that trip also when I saw how joyful the youngsters were and how valuable the experience was for the entire family. The journey started off with the best safari rides I had ever been on. These can and do vary significantly from time to time; the quality is determined by the site and the driver or tracker, by the weather or just plain luck. Then the incident I described earlier ensued, my fall from the van and the ensuing broken ribs. That made things a lot harder for me but we did not lose any travel time or miss a single scheduled site because of it.

Since this was my second trip to several of the places we visited, I did give myself permission in advance to skip a couple of places along the way but there were very few I actually missed. Although it was a struggle some of the time, the memories that my family retain about this trip were worth every minute and every dollar. Although one might not always be aware of the fact from visits to small traditional villages that dot the landscape, South Africa is not really a third world country. It has a good transportation infrastructure, a well developed educational system, quite decent tourist facilities and passable technology. I could have safely availed myself of the medical facilities in one of the large cities to have my injury evaluated but that would have been quite time-taking and inconvenient. And here I am to tell the tale. I am not likely to plan another such taxing undertaking in the near future or sign up for as long a plane ride as I had to endure to get to South Africa although no one knows with any certainty what the days ahead will bring. (Flying first class or business class would ease the stress of a long trip but I would not happily pay five or six times the economy fare. I prefer to donate that money to some worthwhile cause rather than simply increase my sitting comfort for one day.)

The Rest of the World

Folks ask me what places I would travel to now if I could go anywhere I wanted.. Bev and I have never been to Tibet, primarily for political reasons, so I guess I would go there if my medical condition were better and the behavior of the Chinese government more humane. Neither of those eventualities is likely to occur however. Too much climbing and too much altitude to consider that option now. I still remember how difficult it was to become accustomed to La Paz. It is hard to even walk up a hill in that city without huffing and puffing until you are there for a couple of days. Tibet is quite extreme in that respect as well.. I like a lot of oxygen these days. Then there are regions of Indonesia and all of Malaysia that I would like to visit even though I have spent a couple of months in the former country. I missed lots of hill tribe locales in the country sides of Southeast Asia when I traveled there because my days seemed always too few in that fascinating region. I would enjoy exploring more of India where the variety of interesting sites is limitless because four visits to that country were insufficient. On the other hand, locales with vast stretches of mostly uninhabited land mass – Australia, Siberia, Mongolia, much of Canada – are of little interest to me because I much prefer exploring cultures and meeting people rather than gazing at deserts or grasslands or great forests, no matter how beautiful they may be. I would like to visit Madagascar for the wonderful animal life that exists there but it has not been a compelling destination for me. The area of the world where I have never journeyed and would most love to visit is Central Africa but the massive struggles and horrific wars that have transpired there over the past decade or so and which still threaten the inhabitants of the area have kept me away; these conflicts are likely not to diminish very soon. I will certainly never see certain places in the world at this point and I guess I just have to settle for that. The wonderful traditional tribal groups of Ethiopia are now beyond my physical reach as are the isolated peoples in the hills of Irian Jaya, the Indonesian province on the western side of the Island of New Guinea. I will never track the gorillas in Rwanda. There are thousands of bird species and countless other animals I will never view in the wild. By the way, these are statements of fact, not regrets. I have few actual misgivings about any of these facts because I feel I have done what I could to fulfill my travel dreams and I virtually never muse about what I might have done had I started earlier or had more time to spend in a particular place or gone to some area more frequently or had more money to spend. What I have done is take advantage of most of the opportunities I have had and making the best of those chances is a very substantial achievement in my opinion.

I have also discovered over the years that travel is a never ending process. Everywhere I have gone, I have found inspiration to set off to some additional destination because of what I learned from the place I was in or the people I encountered there. I cited a specific instance of this earlier but it has been a recurrent happening. As I stand on some overview looking down on a unique geological formation that inspires wonder in me, the experience also often motivates some nearby observer I have struck up a conversation with to remark that it reminds him or her of (fill in the name or travel site) and I should really see that too. As I witness a time-honored event or ceremony in some foreign cultural setting, the occasion often invokes memories amongst fellow travelers of an equally mysterious or moving occurrence that they have witnessed in another setting entirely. Thus, important travel experiences shared along the way generate ideas for future ventures also and folks with similar interests are inclined to communicate the highlights of their trips to other like-minded travelers. We also often enjoy casual conversations with others who wander about in similar places about our respective everyday lives. As we sit in some small hotel lobby, we chatter about our kids, laugh about our misadventures, tell tales of the places we come from or other locales we have journeyed to. Such dialogue makes for a pleasant bonus at the close of an already enriching day. We have occasionally sustained relationships with folks we have met on our trips for a period of time afterwards although we find these are difficult contacts to keep up when you are a continent or two away from one another.

We Must Be Rich

One of the questions that children sometime ask me when I do a school presentation (especially in the inner city) is "How much did that cost?" spoken with the wide-eyed implication that we must be rich. Adults generally do not make the same inquiry although they probably have a similar assumption in back of their mind as they view places my travels lead me to and the excitement I convey. And perhaps there is a partial truth to that observation. But the main factors that have enabled me to do my explorations are my choices, my values, and even my specific mode of travel. Except for the responsibility of being a father and my deep investment in the profession of education, my highest priority has been a search for adventure, for plumbing the mysteries of the world around me. Our family has lived in the same house for all but the first year or two of my marriage, a house that was relatively inexpensive to start with and is long since paid off. Bev does not buy diamonds or gold to wear, and she surely does not purchase animal fur to keep her body warm in the Philly winters. Neither of us invests much more than necessary in our clothes nor do we have a designer outfit between us insofar as I am aware of. The last time we had anyone's names on our clothes was when we went to work at overnight camps and wanted to make sure our stuff did not disappear in the camp laundry service. Our current cars are respectively six and five years old, modest in size, get good gas mileage and will probably last us until their motors fall out (or until ours do). That is also the history of our past vehicles most of which we bought used. As I mentioned above, almost all of our decorations are inexpensive artifacts from the Third World and our house has had few upgrades over the 48 years we have lived in it. Our furniture includes almost exclusively chairs and tables and beds and bureaus we purchased within a few years after we moved in. Although we do spend money on recreation and eating out, we do not go to restaurants which cost $100.00 or more per couple for fancy dinners in plush settings. We do subscribe to some theaters and orchestra concerts but usually sit in reasonably priced seats as is also true when we attend occasional operas or dance programs or sports events.

So why do I share these personal details? I do so precisely because adults have the same questions as the kids I present my programs to but are usually too self-conscious or "polite" to ask them however much they may be on their mind. The fact is that many readers must be wondering how we have been able to travel so frequently, so far and so independently. It was not inexpensive nor was it financially overwhelming for us to do so but it would not have been possible to do it the way we have if we were poor either. I just want to put that aspect of my travel accurately in the context of my life and my values. Many people can choose to do what we did; most people can do some adventures somewhere some of the time if they decide to take that path.

The overall effect of so many years of travel through the Third World which has taught me so many valuable lessons about varying cultures and offered me so many challenges and adventures, together with reading I have done about other societies, has been to make me a much different person than I would otherwise have been. My appreciation of the endless range of values and cultural practices has made me much more accepting of others and more at one with the greater world in which I live. I feel bound with everyone everywhere to an extent that could never have developed so fully without my travel experiences. Floods in Bangladesh, tsunamis in Thailand and Indonesia, mudslides in Peru and China are all events that touch me personally and deeply as do the creation of animal shelters and anti-poaching programs in Africa and the end of civil wars in Sri Lanka and Africa. I have read with interest some of the great non-English writers from all over the globe whether I have actually visited their country or not. I realize how much I missed in school about the nature of our planet and the people who live on it. I think about, care about, and work to improve the quality of life of my brethren in Asia and Africa, Meso- and South America, the South Pacific and the continent of Europe. Perhaps I would eventually have come to this place without my journeys but I doubt it. Aside from the joy and adventure I have experienced, my personal enrichment in every respect has made it all worthwhile. I am a far better person thanks to my travels. The commitment to help the less fortunate in this world that was born in part from the experience in Acapulco that I related at the beginning of this book has been continually fortified by what I have seen and learned during the many voyages I have undertaken over the past years. The more I understand about the world, the more I feel connected to it and responsible for its welfare.

If the reader wants to travel to some of the places I have written about here, you can probably do your share of that also. Put aside fears and worries, keep yourself in good traveling condition, save some money (drink cheaper wine, hold off on the next car or house upgrade, look for economy flights and hotels on the internet, find opportunity for involvement with groups that send folks abroad on cultural or economic improvement programs if that fits your interests), and take a risk. I cannot guarantee you success but, if you have half the good fortune and enrichment and enjoyment I have had, you will be glad you got started on this endeavor. Good luck!

APPENDIX

- In an article in the Travel Section of the *Philadelphia Inquirer*, Sunday, February,22, 2009, William Echenberger wrote:

  In Sydney, I merely hailed a taxi, opened the door and jumped in the back seat. The driver narrowed his eyes into a suspicious grin. There was a pause. "Where to, mate?" he finally asked in a voice that could chill a refrigerator. In Marrakesh, I simply crossed by legs during an interview with a government official. Immediately, a great hush came over the room. A moment later, my informant remembered an important appointment and excused himself. In a Mumbai restaurant, all I did was reach for the naan bread. A diner at the next table shot me a look of disgust.

  As I was checking out of a Rio De Janeiro hotel, the desk clerk asked, "Did you enjoy your stay with us?" I flashed him an enthusiastic OK sign to indicate that I did. He stalked away, anger surround his face like a vapor.

It took years before I realized what was going on. I had unwittingly committed a faux pas, a gaffe, a breach of etiquette, a social blunder. To varying degrees, I had offended my hosts. My only comfort is my ignorance, and I take solace in Oscar Wilde's observation that a gentleman is someone who never gives offense – unintentionally.

And after nearly 25 years of travel on six continents, I have learned the hard way that getting through customs means more than just filling out a declaration of goods purchased. It means navigating through a serious of cultural booby traps. It means understanding that while people everywhere are the same biologically, they can be worlds apart in their habits and traditions. And so I have advice for anyone visiting another country. Eat, drink – and be wary.

My Australian taxi driver took offense because I sat in the back seat rather than up front, next to him. His attitude, widely shared by his compatriots, is an outgrowth of Australia's origin as a British penal colony, and the prisoners' subsequent dislike of the pretensions of their class-conscious British overseers....

Sometimes I think the easiest thing would be to simply tie my hands behind my back, but even that wouldn't be enough, because there are countless other ways to offend on the road. The entire area of food and drink is a cultural minefield.

When in Asia, for example, never leave your chopsticks upright in your food. As Chin-ning Chu, author of The Asian Mind Game, writes "In the ceremony to honor the dead, many Asians offer food to their deceased ancestors by placing incense in the bowl and burning it as a way to carry the food to the other world. It is a common Asian superstition that to place your chopsticks in such a way is bad luck and means that this meal for the dead rather than the living.

When drinking with others in Prague, the Czechs deem it important before the first sip to look your companion in the eye and lightly clink glasses. Just a couple of hundred miles away in Budapest, however, that identical gesture can get you in deep in goulash. There, the clink is considered unpatriotic, because it was once the signal for a coup.

Even a seemingly gracious gesture like gift-giving is fraught with peril. Although your hosts in China will expect a gift, three items to avoid are clocks, books and umbrellas because they are associated with, respectively, death, defeat and divorce. It has to do with homonyms- words and phrases that sound alike but mean different things.

In Chinese, "giving a clock" sounds like "seeing someone off to his end," "giving a book" comes out as "delivering defeat," and "giving an umbrella" sounds something like "Your family will be dispersed."

Similarly, never give four of anything in Japan because the word for four is the same as the word for death. Indeed, an American golf ball maker experienced sluggish sales in Japan until it realized that it had packaged the product in groups of four.

If you show up with flowers at an Indonesian home, you'll be welcomed warmly. Unless, of course, you *bring chrysanthemums (they're used only for funerals) or if you bring an odd number (it's considered unlucky) Oh, and when your host asks, "Have you eaten?", say yes – even when you're starving. It's a rhetorical, throwaway question (something like "How do you do?") and the answer should always be yes.*

Congratulating an expectant mother can backfire in Kenya – it has one of the world's highest infant mortality rates, and discussing pregnancy is considered bad luck. Wearing a green hat will get you mocked in southern China because it's the sign of an impotent husband (superstition holds that the green-headed tortoise is unable to mate and allows a snake to take its place). Patting someone on the head in Thailand is a major no-no because Thais believe that's where their spirits reside.

There seems to be no end to the number of ways we can offend. When you jet off to an exotic place, you're changing more than time zones. Travel won't be broadening unless your mind is broad to begin with. But, after all, a foreign country isn't designed to make the traveler comfortable – it's designed to make its own people comfortable.

These illustrative examples of cultural differences are just a small assortment of the many variations between groups of people and how they interpret symbols and gestures and both verbal and non-verbal behaviors. The article illustrates some of the things that are helpful for the traveler be aware of as he interacts with folks he meets on his travels.

- In an article posted on AOL on July 6, 2009, William Forman of UP wrote the following:

   URUMQI, China (July 6) - Riots and street battles killed at least 140 people in China's western Xinjiang province and injured 828 others in the deadliest ethnic unrest to hit the region in decades. Officials said Monday the death toll was expected to rise.
   Police sealed off streets in parts of the provincial capital, Urumqi, after discord between ethnic Muslim Uighur people and China's Han majority erupted into violence. Witnesses reported a new, smaller protest Monday in a second city, Kashgar.

   The unrest is another troubling sign for Beijing at how rapid economic development has failed to stem — and even has exacerbated — resentment among ethnic minorities, who say they are being marginalized in their homelands as Chinese migrants pour in.

   Columns of paramilitary police in green camouflage uniforms, helmets and flak vests marched Monday around Urumqi's main bazaar — a largely Uighur neighborhood — carrying batons and shields. Mobile phone service was blocked, and Internet links were also cut or slowed down.

   Rioters on Sunday overturned barricades, attacked vehicles and houses, and clashed violently with police in Urumqi, according to media and witness accounts. State television aired footage showing protesters attacking and kicking people on the ground. Other people, who appeared to be Han Chinese, sat dazed with blood pouring down their faces.

There was little immediate explanation for how so many people died. The government accused a Uighur businesswoman living in the U.S. of inciting the riots through phone calls and "propaganda" spread on Web sites.

Exile groups said the violence started only after police began cracking down on a peaceful protest demanding justice for two Uighurs killed last month during a fight with Han co-workers at a factory in southern China.

Thousands of people took part in Sunday's disturbance, unlike recent sporadic separatist violence carried out by small groups in Xinjiang. The clashes echoed the violent protest that rocked Tibet last year and left many Tibetan communities living under clamped-down security ever since.

Tensions between Uighurs and the majority Han Chinese are never far from the surface in Xinjiang, a sprawling region rich in minerals and oil that borders eight Central Asian nations. Many Uighurs (pronounced WEE-gers) yearn for independence and some militants have waged a sporadic, violent separatist campaign.

Uighurs make up the largest ethnic group in Xinjiang, but not in the capital of Urumqi, which has attracted large numbers of Han Chinese migrants. The city of 2.3 million is now overwhelmingly Chinese — a source of frustration for native Uighurs who say they are being squeezed out.

Kakharman Khozamberdi — leader of a Uighur

political movement in Kazakhstan, where the Uighur minority has its largest presence outside China — said machine gun fire was heard all night long. One witness told Khozamberdi 10 bodies were seen near a bazaar, including those of women and children.

In Geneva, U.N. Secretary-General Ban Ki-moon urged China and any country with violent protests to use extreme care. He urged all government to "protect the life and safety of civilians." About 1,000 to 3,000 Uighur demonstrators had gathered Sunday in the regional capital for a protest that apparently spun out of control. Accounts differed over what happened, but the violence seemed to have started when the crowd of protesters refused to disperse.

The official Xinhua News Agency reported hundreds of people were arrested and checkpoints ringed the city to prevent rioters from escaping. Mobile phone service provided by at least one company was cut Monday to stop people from organizing further action in Xinjiang.

So much for our stalwart Han tourist guide's explanation for the presence of Chinese soldiers along the road in Xinjiang. They were surely not there to prevent a few murders in the desert as we were told.

- In spite of my disinclination to provide a host of specific recommendations for travel, I list here some of the very favorite craft centers I have visited and the objects they specialize in should the reader travel to the designated areas at some time or other. I mentioned above that Bev and I collect necklaces and masks respectively but these are not necessarily the best crafts in a particular locale. Here are a few places we have enjoyed shopping and/or have admired the workmanship. In each place, the items are made by the group of people who pass the designs on through generations and there are good examples of the crafts available at an affordable price.

West and Central Africa: Wooden masks carved in extremely varied and imaginative fashion and representative of the tribal beliefs and traditions; the best place to buy masks anywhere in the world. The Cote d'Ivoire may be the best of the best. Other wood carvings from those areas can be beautiful and most creative as well. Bronze figures representing village scenes and portraying typical residents done in the lost wax method are also attractive and interesting in those areas. These are wonderful items for a shelf or table at home. Woven cloths including colorful Kente Cloth from Ghana and Mudcloth from Djenne, Mali are highly desirable. In the Cote D'Ivoire and on the Western side of the continent, very nice Batik paintings are good choices.

Papua New Guinea: The second most exciting locale to purchase a wide variety of masks most of which represent the spirits worshipped by residents of the jungle; these are quite varied and may be made out of wood or vines or other items from the jungle. Other spirit based, traditional items are carved throughout the area.

India: The richest source of fine handiwork anywhere. My favorite crafts are the poured metal objects created by the tribal peoples. These are hard to find most places but they are the most interesting traditional crafts in the country. The silverwork, especially necklaces and bracelets, are outstanding. Other worthwhile crafts include the classical miniature paintings whose tradition goes back several hundred years, the marble crafts which are available in the stores of Agra and the lovely jewelry done by Tibetans and others in the north of the country.

Weaving: There are several kinds of woven goods which have impressed me on my travels. Perhaps the finest of all were the very beautiful cloth pieces created by the Indians who live in and around the amazing market town of Tarabuco, Bolivia high up in the Andes. Equally outstanding are the Ikat cloths of Indonesia which vary from area to area and can be found on many of the islands. There are also some very fine woven goods in Southeast Asia, especially in Vietnamese hill villages and in the towns of Laos. One of the rarest forms of weaving takes place in a few villages on Lake Inle, Myanmar where scarves and other items are created using the threads inside the lotus flower stem. Fine lace work exists in several places. Turkey is an especially good place for this craft as is Romania.

Laquerware: Vietnam and Myanmar feature extremely fine laquer work. One can find practically everything from tables to plates to large pieces of furniture in those countries and the handiwork is extremely painstaking and artistic.

Incidentals: Each area of the world has its specialties though the quality of the work may not be of the highest standard. Mexico offers some very good mask choices although they do not tend to be as imaginative as in some other places. Guatemala has some excellent weavings; a great variety of these can be found in the market of Chichicastenango; others in the villages around Lake Atitlan. Some of the Thankgas of Nepal or North India can be quite artistic. In China and Thailand there are quite lovely creations made of animal bone or ivory, usually depictions of Buddhist figures. The actual list is endless for the shopper/tourist.

Please contact the author at
travelshow@aol.com.

Website: *www.travellectures.com*